Thousand Oaks & Westlake Village

A CONTEMPORARY PORTRAIT

The Thousand Oaks–Westlake Village Regional Chamber of Commerce
and Community Communications, Inc. would like to thank the following companies
for their leadership during the development of this book.

CALIFORNIA SPINE INSTITUTE

The Thousand Oaks–Westlake Village Regional Chamber of Commerce and
Community Communications, Inc. would like to thank the following companies
for their patronage.

The Home Depot
Michael-Thomas Escrow
TempLiving, Inc.

Thousand Oaks & Westlake Village

A CONTEMPORARY PORTRAIT

Written by **PAM BAKER** *Corporate Profiles by* **JIM DUNHAM** *Featuring the photography of* **JOHN EDER, THE STEVEN DUFFEY GROUP**

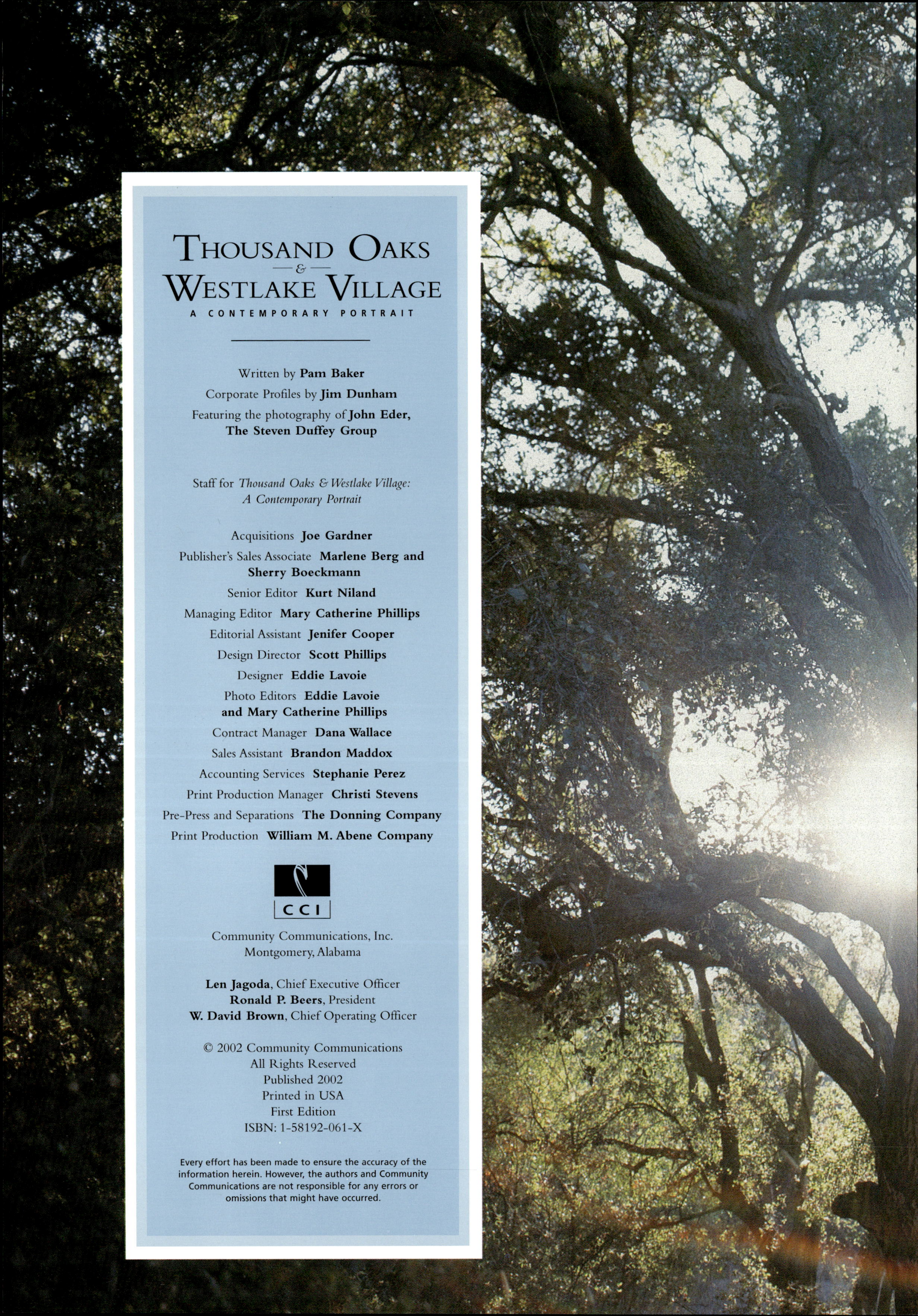

Thousand Oaks & Westlake Village

A CONTEMPORARY PORTRAIT

Written by **Pam Baker**
Corporate Profiles by **Jim Dunham**
Featuring the photography of **John Eder, The Steven Duffey Group**

Staff for *Thousand Oaks & Westlake Village: A Contemporary Portrait*

Acquisitions **Joe Gardner**
Publisher's Sales Associate **Marlene Berg and Sherry Boeckmann**
Senior Editor **Kurt Niland**
Managing Editor **Mary Catherine Phillips**
Editorial Assistant **Jenifer Cooper**
Design Director **Scott Phillips**
Designer **Eddie Lavoie**
Photo Editors **Eddie Lavoie and Mary Catherine Phillips**
Contract Manager **Dana Wallace**
Sales Assistant **Brandon Maddox**
Accounting Services **Stephanie Perez**
Print Production Manager **Christi Stevens**
Pre-Press and Separations **The Donning Company**
Print Production **William M. Abene Company**

CCI

Community Communications, Inc.
Montgomery, Alabama

Len Jagoda, Chief Executive Officer
Ronald P. Beers, President
W. David Brown, Chief Operating Officer

Published 2002
Printed in USA
First Edition
ISBN: 1-58192-061-X

Photo by John Eder

TABLE OF CONTENTS

Photo by John Eder

—3—

An Economic Celebration
Page 34

Attractive to more than just residents seeking a good life, the Thousand Oaks and Westlake Village area has also enticed prominent businesses in nearly every industry. The area's low crime rate and qualified work force are just two of the many reasons companies find the region so alluring.

—4—

Mind, Body & Spirit
Page 40

Variety and quality are the two words most used to describe the Conejo Valley's range of health care, education, and religious institutions. The health care system is large, and nationally known, while offering a complete assortment of services. The region's schools are award-winners in academics as well as sports, while the 100 plus places of worship serve the community's spiritual needs.

—1—

History & Leaders
Page 14

From the early days of Spanish occupation to serving as a popular location for motion pictures, Thousand Oaks and Westlake Village have long been recognized for their natural beauty and surrounding scenery. The two cities together share an illustrious past and a brilliant future.

—5—

Let Us Entertain You
Page 50

The Thousand Oaks and Westlake Village communities are not lacking when it comes to enjoying the arts. Residents can stroll the Gardens of the World or take in an art exhibit or a frontier museum then support a local theatre production. Nationally recognized shows and entertainers frequently visit the area, appearing in such lovely venues as the Thousand Oaks Civic Arts Plaza.

—2—

Urban Landscapes
Page 24

The residents of Thousand Oaks and Westlake Village enjoy an unparalleled quality of life, from thriving and amenable places of employment, to a variety of shops, restaurants, and leisure activities. However, preserving the area's natural charm is a priority for the residents and city governments alike.

—6—

The Sporting Life
Page 60

If the weather is just too nice to be indoors shopping or seeing a show, numerous outdoor activities such as hiking, fishing, riding horses, or playing ball are available year round. With sea and mountains, lakes, and deserts all nearby, the opportunities are limitless. With special centers for youth and senior adults, everyone has a chance to play.

Photo by John Eder

FOREWORD

A quality, culturally diverse family environment; a winning spirit; an educational powerhouse; and an ideal home for business. That's the Thousand Oaks-Westlake Village area.

It's an exciting time in Thousand Oaks and Westlake Village. Those of us who live here know and appreciate the warmth and friendliness of our people, respect our traditions and heritage, take pride in sheer natural beauty of our surroundings, and look forward to many opportunities for a prosperous future.

On behalf of the Thousand Oaks-Westlake Village Regional Chamber of Commerce and its local businesses, we present this book to our community.

Within these beautiful pages, it is our sincere hope that you will experience the quality, texture, and healthy pulse of these dynamic cities. We are rich in wonderful people, progressive partnerships, and exciting opportunities. As you enjoy this book, you will come to understand why our future is so bright.

We are proud to share with you a glimpse into the heart and soul of Thousand Oaks and Westlake Village-cities in the midst of remarkable successes in the new millennium and, more simply, great places to live, work, and do business. Most of all, however, Thousand Oaks and Westlake Village are places simply to enjoy.

The Thousand Oaks-Westlake Village
Regional Chamber of Commerce

Photo by John Eder

PREFACE

As a journalist and author, I travel the world over quite frequently. I never tire of meeting new people and seeing new places. But seldom do I actually want to stay in any one place forever. Thousand Oaks-Westlake Village, though, has stolen my heart and I could easily live there happily ever after.

The entire area is charming, warm, and welcoming. When the cities were planned, the founders knew exactly what touches to add to the masterpiece to build a version of nirvana that was both obtainable and sustainable. I've never seen a more successful planned community, or one as unique and personable. There are no cookie-cutter approaches to architecture, lifestyle, or opinions in Thousand Oaks-Westlake Village!

Many thanks to everyone in both cities. Thanks for your help, encouragement, and a really wonderful time! But a special thanks goes to the folks at the Thousand Oaks-Westlake Village Regional Chamber of Commerce. All this time, Southerners—like me—thought we had the market cornered on hospitality, gentility, and grace. We were wrong; you guys are simply the best.

I thank each and every one of you for allowing me the honor of writing your story.

Thanks also to everyone at Community Communications who made this book so wonderful and so gorgeous. To my kids, Stephanie and Ben Baker, thanks once again for your understanding and patience while I was working under deadline despite your own pressures as you, Stephanie, prepared for your freshman year at college, and you, Ben, prepared for your senior year in high school. I'm proud of you both.

To the Steven Duffey Group, thanks as always for the beautiful photographs that illustrate this book, and to Steven himself, my beloved brother, thanks for being you, for working by my side and putting up with the craziness. To my mother and father, Nana and Wade Duffey, thanks for the encouragement and all your help. They taught me to travel with an open mind, a gracious heart, and a curious eye.

Although this is not an authoritative work, it is a largely accurate popular telling. If there are errors or omissions, God forbid, such is entirely accidental and I ask your forgiveness. For the parts that are perfect and right, I thank God and the people of Thousand Oaks-Westlake Village for creating a perfect place on earth and a story well worth the telling!

Good luck to you all,
Pam Baker

Part One

CHAPTER ONE

—— 1 ——

History & Leaders

Lake Sherwood, named from the area's extensive use in the 1922 movie *Robin Hood*, offers unparalleled sporting activities as well as a pastoral environment for relaxation. Photo by John Eder

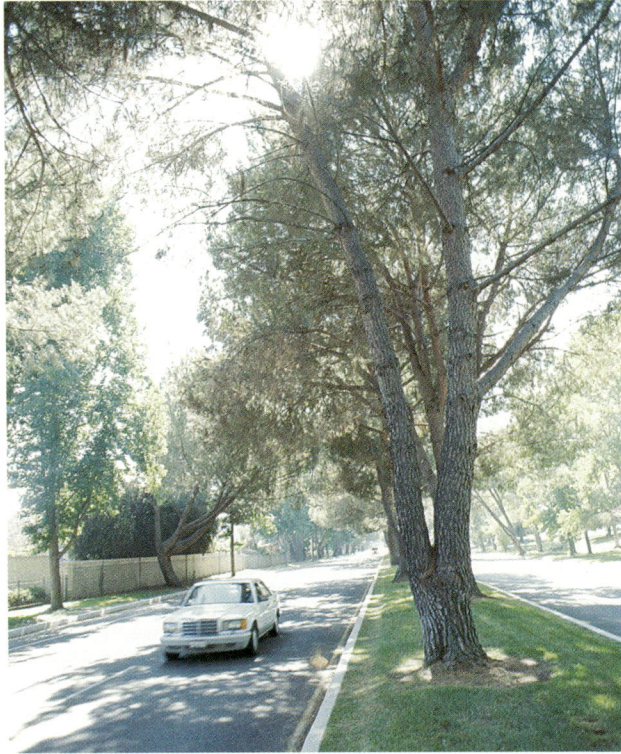

(above) Agoura Road in Westlake Village typifies the calm beauty of the Thousand Oaks-Westlake Village area. Photo by John Eder

(below) A popular activity for both health and outdoors fanatics, bike riding is a sport seemingly tailor-made for the sunny weather and lush landscape of the Thousand Oaks and Westlake Village area. Photo by John Eder

The Conejo Valley is home to the prosperous and thriving communities of Thousand Oaks and Westlake Village. It is surrounded by countryside that is nearly as tranquil and pristine as it was when Spanish settlers arrived in the 1800s.

Nine miles inland from the Pacific Ocean, both cities sit 900 feet above sea level at the Ventura/Los Angeles County line, about halfway between the cities of Los Angeles and Santa Barbara.

Thousand Oaks and Westlake Village together cover about 62 square miles. They are suburbs of the city of Los Angeles which sprawls a little over 30 miles to the west. The two neighbors are planned communities built along both sides of U.S. Highway 101, locally called the Ventura Freeway.

Thousand Oaks and Westlake Village are the predominant economic engines in the area, but the unincorporated areas of Newbury Park and Lake Sherwood add significantly to the overall community. Newbury Park was named for the area's first postmaster Egbert Starr Newbury. The word "park" was added to the name because of the many trees in the area. Lake Sherwood is three miles south of Thousand Oaks. In 1889, the lake was called Canterbury Lake. The name was changed to Lake Mathiessen in 1898 to honor its new owner, F. W. Mathiessen, Jr. In 1922, the name changed to its current moniker because of the extensive use of the area in filming *Robin Hood.*

The first recorded history of the Thousand Oaks-Westlake Village area dates back to 1542 when explorer Juan Rodriguez Cabrillo discovered Alta, California. He anchored in several harbors along the way from San Diego to Point Conception, placing his country's flag

at Point Mugu and claiming the land for the King of Spain. Once claimed, the land rested undisturbed until the Spanish returned in the 1700s.

Captain Gasper de Portola and his party of Spanish explorers and missionaries traveled north, on what is now called the El Camino Real, in 1770. These travelers camped near present day Westlake Village, which, at the time, was a Chumash Indian village. Their route is marked today by a series of mission bells, several of which can be seen along the 101 corridor in the Conejo Valley.

The chaplain of the expedition, Father Juan Crespi, wrote in his journal: "We are on a plain of considerable extent and much beauty, forested on all parts by live oaks and oak trees, with much pasturage and water." The scene resembled the much imagined promised land of milk and honey, sunshine, and sea.

A Spanish governor granted over 48,000 acres of land to two loyal soldiers. One of the grants covered the area now called Conejo Valley. For nearly a half a century, cattle herds grazed the land with vaqueros tending the stock. As colorful as the tales are of vaquero life, the political scene was even more so. Mexico won independence from Spain in 1821 and California became a Mexican territory. The land was parceled into ranchos by government grants. Present day Westlake Village sits on a portion of two of those grants, Rancho El Conejo and Rancho Las Virgenes. In 1850, California was admitted into the union (U.S.) and most of the land now known as Ventura County was divided among only 19 families. A post office and the historic Stagecoach Inn, a stop on the stagecoach route between Los Angeles and San Francisco, were opened in Thousand Oaks. These historical structures are still standing today.

(above) Concerned for the surroundings their children's children would enjoy, Thousand Oaks city officials created over 14,000 acres of open space nearly 30 years ago. This open space has worked to preserve scenic and natural resources. Photo by John Eder

(below) The Thousand Oaks City Seal depicts the City's association with the County of Ventura and the State of California, as well as the esteemed (and protected) Oak trees found throughout the community. Photo courtesy of the Thousand Oaks-Westlake Village Regional Chamber of Commerce

(above) **The City of Westlake Village seal represents the best parts of the area: sun, sea, mountains, learning, and recreation, all surrounded by lush vegetation. Photo by John Eder**

(below) **With natural beauty, architectural wonders, and a nearby award-winning golf course, the Lake Sherwood area is an attractive place to live and play. Photo by John Eder**

In 1881, the Russell brothers bought a huge parcel of the land (now part of Westlake Village) to use for cattle ranching. To this day the area is known as Russell Ranch although the land was sold to William Randolph Hearst in 1925 and to Fred Albertson in 1943. The Russell family leased back part of the land to continue cattle ranching while the Albertson Company used the remaining acres to produce movies. Among movies and television shows filmed on location were *Robin Hood*, *King Rat*, *Laredo*, *Tarzan*, *Buck Rogers*, *Gunsmoke*, and *Bonanza*.

In the early 1900s, the Janss family bought 10,000 acres of Conejo farmland that would later become Thousand Oaks. The family was the developer of several Southern California subdivisions. By the time the first local highway was built, residents and tourists traveling from Los Angeles were treated to scenic miles of field crops, orchards, and chicken, hog, and dairy farms throughout the countryside. By mid-century, the Janss Corporation activated plans to build a total community. Within ten years, two shopping centers, an industrial park, schools, churches, and a four-year liberal arts college, California Lutheran University, added to the area's allure.

So did Goebel's Lion Farm (later called Jungleland) which opened in 1927 to the delight of locals and tourists alike. Scenes from *Birth Of A Nation*, *Tarzan*, and *The Adventures of Robin Hood*, were filmed on the site often using animals from Jungleland.

The City of Thousand Oaks incorporated in 1964, so named in recognition of the abundance of majestic oak trees in the area. Today it is home for more than 120,000 people. From its beginning, Thousand Oaks has been dedicated to preserving its scenic ambiance and natural resources. More than 14,000 acres with over 75 miles of trails have been preserved as "open space" that allows residents to savor the same natural beauty that mesmerized the Chumash Native Americans hundreds of years ago. Newbury Park also offers miles of trails and natural environment integrated among its neighborhoods.

The American-Hawaiian Steamship Company bought the 12,000 acre Russell Ranch in 1963 for $32 million and, with partner Prudential Insurance Company, commissioned a master plan to design "a city in the country" to be named Westlake Village. The nationally acclaimed model for the planned community concept was designed and built by prominent architects, engineers, and land planners. Westlake Village has since been recognized as one of America's most successful suburbs and finest areas in which to live and work.

Today, Westlake Village is a beautiful, natural environment with award-winning neighborhoods, thriving businesses, and enviable lifestyles for over 8,500 residents. The Los Angeles and Ventura County lines diagonally carved the original Westlake Village in two. The Los Angeles County side (3,456 acres) was incorporated as the City of Westlake Village in 1981. It became the 82nd municipality in the county. The remaining 8,544 acres of the original Russell Ranch, on the Ventura County side, were annexed into the City of Thousand Oaks in two portions: one annexed in 1968, the other in 1972.

The two cities share a beginning and a future. Although the cities have distinct identities, the overall community is dedicated to integrating effective planning, economic vitality, citizen involvement, and a community conscience to enhance and maintain an envious family lifestyle for all residents. 🏇

> **"T**he rich history of the city of Thousand Oaks has provided the area's businesses with a wealth of tradition and numerous success stories. While there were several locations in mind to establish the California Spine Institute, we chose Thousand Oaks for its natural beauty, centralized location, and dynamic and engaging community. The visual aspect of the city of Thousand Oaks and the emerging biotechnological corridor along Highway 101 complement our goal at the Institute quite nicely. We are honored to be a vital part of this invigorating and exciting area.

Dr. John C. Chiu
Chief of Neurospine Surgery
California Spine Institute
California Center for Minimally Invasive Surgery

The 14,000 acres of preserved "open space" ensure that the area's scenic beauty and natural resources will be enjoyed by present and future residents as much as they were by past generations. Photo by John Eder

The natural beauty of the Thousand Oaks-Westlake Village area is particularly evident during springtime when the blossoms are numerous. Photo by John Eder

(above) With such natural beauty, it's easy to see why Thousand Oaks has received the Trail Town USA Hall of Fame award as well as being a recognized "Tree City USA." Photo by John Eder

(opposite) The Gardens of the World, a gift from the Hogan Family Foundation, includes French, Japanese, and California mission gardens as well as an old-fashioned bandstand and grassy amphitheater. Photo by John Eder

CHAPTER TWO

— 2 —

Urban Landscapes

This photo taken from a ridge which borders the Santa Monica Mountains National Recreational Area provides a stunning view of Thousand Oaks and Westlake Village. Photo courtesy of the Thousand Oaks-Westlake Village Regional Chamber of Commerce

While full of rural charm, Thousand Oaks and Westlake Village are havens of city sophistication. Winding roads like this one lie within easy reach of shopping malls, office complexes, and restaurants. Photo by John Eder

Thousand Oaks and Westlake Village are attractive cities for many reasons. Both are widely acclaimed to be among the finest residential areas in Southern California and are consistently ranked among the safest in the nation by FBI reporting standards. The climate is mild with average temperatures ranging between 65-75 degrees in the summer and 53-69 degrees in the winter. Rainfall averages 14.98 inches annually.

Population studies reveal that residents predominantly consist of individuals and families who tend to rank family values and quality of life issues high on their list of priorities. The area's wide streets are clearly marked with unobtrusive wooden signs and lined with bicycle lanes and flowering shrubbery. Most homes are made of concrete or stucco and topped with red Spanish tile roofing. The yards are immaculately groomed; the homes individually styled. Some of the neighborhoods are zoned to accommodate horses. Although clearly suburban in nature, many homes are uniquely designed.

Demographic data indicates that the majority of the local labor force lives within 20 miles of the area and fewer residents are making the 30-mile plus commute to Los Angeles. Educational levels and household incomes have steadily increased and the local economy remains strong.

The number of professionals living in the area has risen as well. According to 2000 U.S. Census data, over 40 percent of residents are employed as executives or professionals, and economists predict the percentage will steadily increase over the next few years. The combination of ample job opportunities, excellent educational systems, and a progressive, diverse business community is an ideal environment for many established and rising professionals.

Attractive professional office complexes throughout the area feature a myriad of amenities, including water ponds and streams, wildlife, trees and gardens, outdoor eating areas, spacious interior work areas, and ample off-street parking. Efficiency, productivity, and economic growth are balanced by a "community conscience" that equally values quality of life. This lifestyle is, in part, achieved through proactive conservation efforts and an abundance of human services.

However, quality of life issues extend beyond work amenities and community services. There are plenty of opportunities for relaxation, dining, shopping, and family fun.

Many informal restaurants flourish in the area and offer menus ranging from fast food to traditional fare from other parts of the country. Chowders, crabcakes, lobsters, southern fried chicken, barbecue ribs, Cajun, Creole, Tex-Mex, Southwestern, Midwestern, and Pacific dishes all are served daily at a variety of places.

Because the population is so diverse, there are also several restaurants that cater to international tastes and offer culinary treats from Mexico, China, Japan, Thailand, Polynesia, France, Italy, Greece, and other Mediterranean countries.

For a more romantic setting, The Landing at Westlake Lake and Marina is a good choice. It has several restaurants serving everything from continental fare and sushi to French and Italian cuisine. Some offer elegant ambiances of white linen dressed tables and fine art with exquisitely presented delectables. Others offer meals in a casual outdoor atmosphere under patio umbrellas amongst charming, waddling ducks and tropical greenery.

There is ample variety in shops throughout the area as well. Local shoppers are casual yet savvy and sophisticated. Variety, quality, and value top their shopping lists.

Thousand Oaks Boulevard bisects the area from east to west and is a busy shopping corridor with the world's largest auto mall: the Thousand Oaks Auto Mall. Vehicles of every description from 32 separate franchises and 15 dealers are represented. Family-owned businesses, the Thousand Oaks Civic Arts Plaza and the Gardens of the World also have a strong presence on the "Boulevard," capped on one end by the Westlake Village Marketplace and the other end by the Oaks Regional Shopping Mall.

The Oaks Regional Shopping Mall has 160 specialty shops, a movie complex, food court, restaurants, and major department stores. Midway down the boulevard, the smaller European-style Northgate Plaza and the Promenade at Westlake shopping centers face each other at the intersection of Westlake Boulevard and Thousand Oaks Boulevard. Both feature chic specialty stores and restaurants housed in Mediterranean-style structures among flowers. The Promenade additionally boasts a movie complex, sculptures, water features, and live entertainment is occasionally offered on the weekends.

(above) The Promenade at Westlake is a European-style shopping center at the intersection of Westlake Boulevard and Thousand Oaks Boulevard. It boasts not only specialty stores and restaurants, but a movie complex, as well as live entertainment on weekends. Photo by John Eder

(below) The only thing better than a huge shopping mall is a huge auto mall! The world's largest is the Thousand Oaks Auto Mall, which tempts buyers with vehicles from 32 separate franchises and 15 dealers. Photo by John Eder

(above) **Northgate Plaza, across the street from the Promenade at Westlake, shows just how attractive a shopping center can be when it is integrated into the look and feel of the community. Photo by John Eder**

(below) **Shopping is both easily accessible and fun with so many merchants to choose from. The Westlake Village Marketplace is one of the more popular shopping venues in the area. Photo by John Eder**

Neighboring North Ranch Mall, also a smaller shopping center, offers shoppers a supermarket, drugstore, specialty shops, and restaurants. Evergreen Plaza, Palm Plaza, and a scattering of other smaller shopping centers also line the Boulevard.

Plans call for additional development along the center of the Boulevard next to City Hall. The proposed 48,000-square-foot park-like complex will include restaurants, shops, a plaza, amphitheater, clock tower, two ponds, ice skating rink, and a movie theater. The project is expected to complement the Thousand Oaks Civic Arts Plaza and Gardens of the World—an internationally inspired community park across the street, which will create a town-center atmosphere.

Traveling the Conejo Valley's shopping route begins with one of Westlake Village's original shopping centers, The County Line. This quaint center features a movie house that is reminiscent of a time before mega-movie complexes. The Westlake Village Marketplace is north of the freeway on Lindero Canyon. This premier Westlake center features a variety of big-name chain stores, eateries, and shopping for hobby enthusiasts. Westlake Plaza, on the south side of the Ventura freeway on Westlake Boulevard, has a selection of men's, women's, and children's clothing and shoe stores, a camera shop, restaurants, and a drugstore. Nearby is the Vons/Sav-on Center with a variety of grocery and drugstore goods, a coffee shop, and eateries. Gelson's Market Plaza has a grocery store, fine jewelry, an art dealer, and other specialty shops.

As mentioned earlier, the Promenade and the Northgate Plaza sit on either side of Westlake Boulevard at Thousand Oaks Boulevard. Across the Boulevard is North Ranch Mall which features financial

institutions, grocery stores (some featuring natural products), and other unique home and clothing stores.

Continuing along the shopping route is the Evergreen Plaza, the Palm Plaza, and a scattering of other small shopping centers too numerous to name, but each worthy of a visit. The recently renovated Janss Marketplace is also a popular shopping center with well known anchoring stores and a variety of specialty stores. It has a nine-screen Cineplex and is surrounded by neighboring restaurants and fast food establishments. Other popular stores are nearby.

Although new housing and stores are seemingly always springing up throughout the area, Thousand Oaks and Westlake Village have retained their original charm. Billboards do not exist, neither does graffiti, and utility lines are buried underground in Westlake Village. The city of Thousand Oaks has purchased land, as have private citizens, to protect the area from overdevelopment. Smart growth and balance in the quality of life overall are the key motivators behind economic development strategies in the area. 🐾

(above) The Oaks Shopping Center covers 90 acres and consists of 103 million square feet. Shoppers can find traditional department stores, famous eateries, and numerous specialty stores. Its main focus is to provide the community with quality shopping and convenience. Photo compliments of The Oaks Shopping Center

(left) A romantic choice for fine fare, the Landing offers meals of many different styles served in settings ranging from elegantly dressed white linen tables and fine art to casual outdoors dining under patio umbrellas. Photo by John Eder

The multitude of food choices makes eating out a fun time of exploration. The Rosti Italian Restaurant of Westlake Village entices diners who seek authentic Italian food. Photo by John Eder

Residents of the Thousand Oaks-Westlake Village area have a plethora of choices for entertainment including one timeless option—the big screen. Photo courtesy of the Thousand Oaks-Westlake Village Regional Chamber of Commerce

CHAPTER THREE

—— 3 ——

An Economic Celebration

Many businesses are attracted to the Thousand Oaks-Westlake Village area because their employees can enjoy a safe environment, lower taxes, and develop working skills in a professional environment. Photo by John Eder

Thousand Oaks and Westlake Village are planned communities where every street was designed and every amenity built with a purpose. That is not to say that the cities are without originality; nothing could be further from the truth. Unlike other suburban areas, the homes here are not repetitive or redundant, each differs from its neighbors in design, and each neighborhood has a personality borne from a wide variety of individual aesthetic touches. It is not a "cookie-cutter" approach to living, it's just that the citizens care enough to tend to the details. The result is a harmonious and enticing atmosphere. So it is of no big surprise that the cities have enjoyed a unique opportunity to be selective about the makeup and mix of the local business community as well.

The Highway 101 corridor, in particular, which passes through Westlake Village, Thousand Oaks, and Newbury Park has become a highly desirable location for businesses seeking sanctuary from high taxes and crime rates in Los Angeles. A large and talented labor pool is also attractive to new and existing businesses. More than 60,000 people over the age of 16 are in a workforce located within a 20-mile radius of the Conejo Valley. Within this group, nearly 90 percent have completed high school and over 35 percent hold a bachelor's degree or higher. Forty percent are in management or professional careers and 32 percent are in sales or administrative occupations.

Additional business development advantages in the area include attractive commercial facilities, available at competitive rents, and a highly desirable quality of life and school systems that help to recruit and retain employees.

Many of the companies enjoying an address in the two cities along the Highway 101 corridor hail from high-tech industries. Their presence has shaped the corridor into one of the top 50 metropolitan areas in the United States for technology output. The corridor dominated the 2000 list of finalists, 20 companies out of a total of

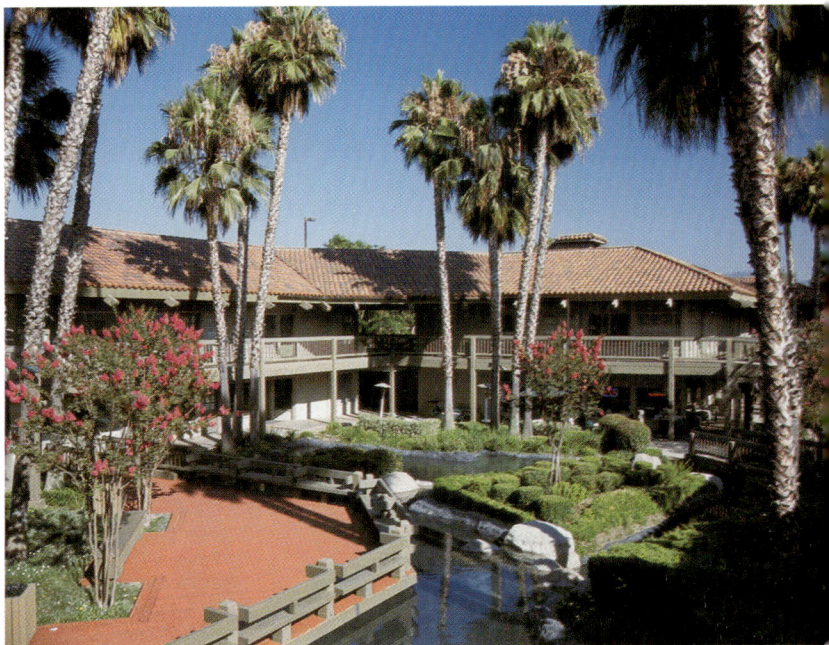

50, on Deloitte & Touches's list of the fastest-growing technology companies in the Los Angeles area.

Telecommunications, Internet, biomedical, and interactive technology companies add sufficient diversity to keep the area economically strong. Far from just a laundry list of local employers, the names of the companies either headquartered or present in the area reads like a Who's Who list from a variety of industries. This is not only a reflection on the business acumen, but on the strengths of the Thousand Oaks-Westlake Village Regional Chamber of Commerce and local governments in attracting and maintaining a stable and prosperous economic foundation.

Among the high-tech, biotech, and computer employers in the area are Amgen, the largest biomedical/genetics company in the world and the county's largest private employer, and Rockwell International, a leading manufacturer of industrial automation equipment and aviation/communications equipment. Other big-name

(left) The Thousand Oaks transit depot provides workers an alternative way to navigate their way to and from their place of employment. The transit system ultimately allows for fewer cars to be on the road during peak traffic hours, thus making a shorter commute. Photo by John Eder

(below) Dole Food Company, the world's largest grower and supplier of fruits, vegetables, and nuts, realizes the benefits that come with locating their world headquarters in Westlake Village. Photo by John Eder

companies on the corridor include Skyworks, Trompeter Electronics, Inc., Baxter Pharmaceutical, United Online Inc., General Dynamics Electronic Systems, Autologic, Adelphia, Condor Pacific Industries, Agilent Technologies, Surfware, Inc., and INTEL, Inc.

Major employers in the communications industry include Verizon California and Ventura County Star.

In the service industry, leading local employers include WellPoint Health Network, one of the nation's largest publicly traded managed care companies; Farmer's Insurance Company; the City of Thousand Oaks; and J.D. Powers and Associates.

Among manufacturing and distributing companies are Jafra Cosmetics International, RVL Packaging, Parker Symetrics, Inc., W.S. Shamban & Company, MWS Wire Products, Condor Pacific Industries, Inc., K-Swiss Athletic Footwear, and Right Start Stores, Inc. Dole Food Company, the world's largest grower and supplier of fresh and packaged fruits, juices, vegetables, and nuts, has its world headquarters in Westlake Village.

The Thousand Oaks-Westlake Village area leads the county in retail sales activity. Consumers from adjacent communities are attracted to the wide array of retail amenities.

With a strong base of competitive businesses, quality of life, and sense of community, Thousand Oaks and Westlake Village are well situated for growth and prosperity for future generations. ❧

With the variety of businesses and shops in the area, residents are easily able to find goods and services to meet their daily needs. Keeping business in the area provides more jobs to citizens in Thousand Oaks and Westlake Village while stabilizing the economy. Photo by John Eder

CHAPTER FOUR

4

Mind, Body & Spirit

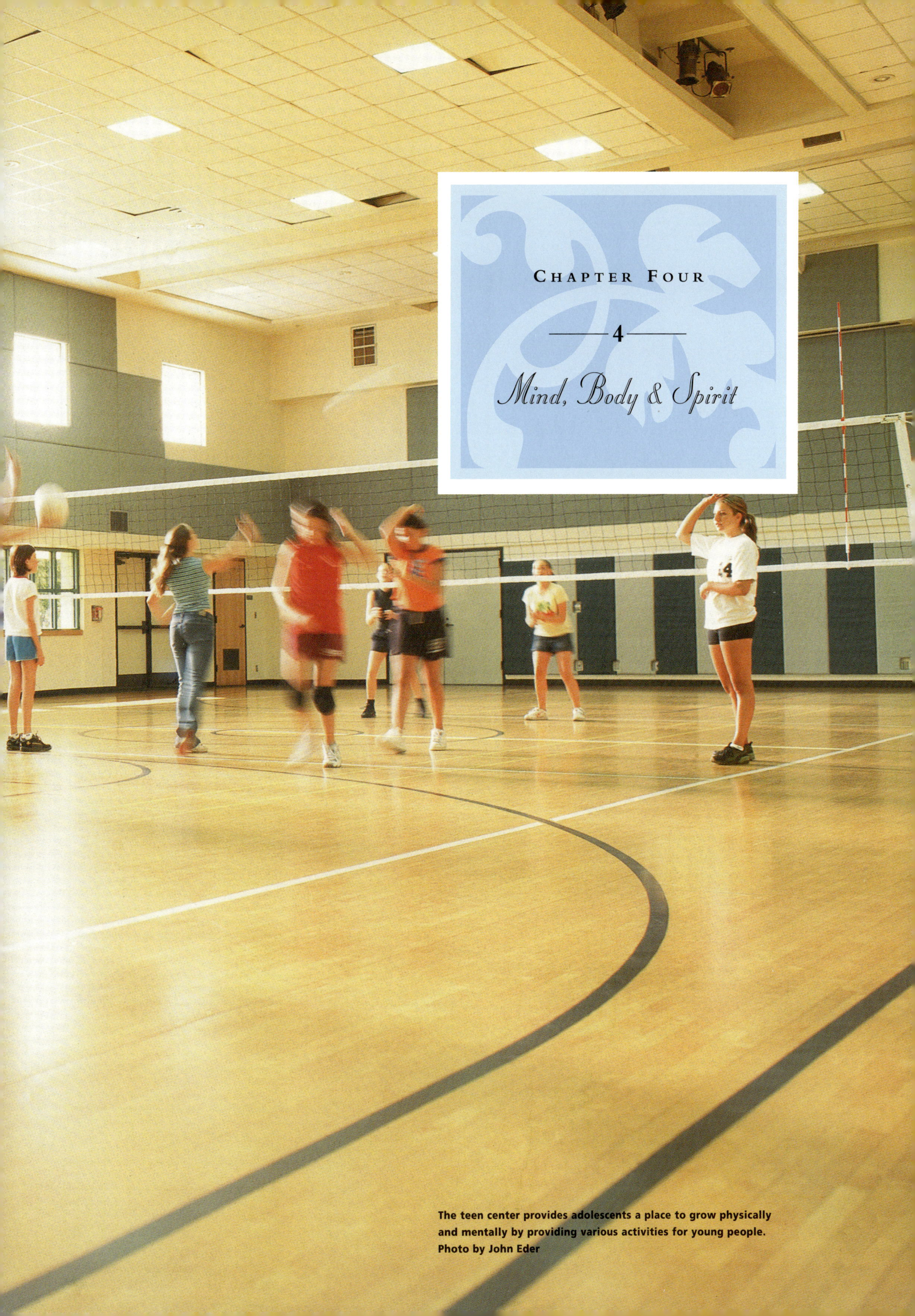

The teen center provides adolescents a place to grow physically and mentally by providing various activities for young people. Photo by John Eder

Being healthy takes hard work and dedication, both of which Conejo Valley residents have in abundance, making this area the healthiest in California. Photo by John Eder

Conejo Valley residents are among the healthiest in the state according to county statistics compiled by the state of California. Many individuals attribute this general condition of wellness to the community's clean air, mild climate, open spaces, and recreational opportunities. It is not uncommon for new residents to cite a desire for a healthier environment among their top five reasons for moving to Thousand Oaks and Westlake Village.

Of course, part of the reason local residents tend to be healthy is the outstanding healthcare services offered in the area. Excellent healthcare providers in a variety of medical and dental fields have practices in Thousand Oaks and Westlake Village. Virtually no medical treatment or technique is missing from the list of services offered by the local medical community.

Los Robles Regional Medical Center in Thousand Oaks is the communities' primary institution for hospital care. The former Westlake Village Hospital is now an Urgent Care Center specializing in emergency services.

The acute care Los Robles Regional Medical Center has served Ventura County for over 30 years and is accredited by the Joint Commission of Accreditation of Health Care Organizations. It offers 24-hour emergency service and a variety of other services including the Los Robles SurgiCenter, Thousand Oaks Radiology and Breast

Center, Conejo Medical Magnetic Resonance Systems, the Nutrition Clinic, North Oaks Radiation, and the Conejo Renal Center. Additionally, Los Robles Heart Center is nationally renown for cardiac care.

The hospital has two locations with more than 400 physicians on staff representing more than 30 specialties. Among its many medical services are intensive and critical care units, maternity, neonatal intensive care, medical and surgical care units, comprehensive cancer center, home care, operating rooms, same day surgery, transitional care unit, rehabilitation center, senior care, behavioral health, and a pain management center.

Since education is important in preventing and treating illness and injury, Los Robles also provides numerous free health classes on a variety of topics.

Another important factor behind Thousand Oaks and Westlake Village's family values and attention to balance is the presence of a diverse and thriving religious community. There are over 100 places of worship throughout the area.

Adding to the area's allure are the exceptional school systems: the Conejo Valley Unified School District (CVUSD) and the Las Virgenes Unified School District (LVUSD). Headquartered in Thousand Oaks, the CVUSD operates four high schools, four intermediate, and 19

(above) Wildwood Park and other natural parks and facilities offer healthy recreational options. Photo by John Eder

(below) The Conejo Valley Unified School District is an exceptional school system that operates 16 Distinguished California Schools and four National Blue Ribbon Schools. Photo by John Eder

(above) The Health Services Academy is a unique educational opportunity for students at Thousand Oaks High School. Students are able to get a glimpse at a potential medical career while also learning through a hands-on approach. Photo by John Eder

(below) Children learn about personal safety and the danger of strangers through volunteers in the public service arena that offer constant assistance to the community in order to make Thousand Oaks-Westlake Village a safer place. Photo by John Eder

elementary schools. Sixteen have been named Distinguished California Schools while three elementary schools and one intermediate school have been named National Blue Ribbon Schools.

White Oak Elementary School, Lindero Canyon Middle School, and Agoura High School in Westlake Village are in the Las Virgenes Unified School District (LVUSD) since the schools are located across the Los Angeles County line. They too are National Blue Ribbon Schools and California Distinguished Schools.

Both school districts provide "school-to-career" programs. Newbury Park High has the Technical Resource Academic Institute, which academically supports students interested in careers in technology. The Health Services Academy at Thousand Oaks High adds educational enhancement for students interested in entering nursing, radiology, and EMT fields. Westlake High School's Westlake Information Technology also teaches students critical skills necessary for careers in technology. Agoura High School offers similar programs to students as well, such as its highly praised Regional Occupational Program.

Both districts also have a wide ethnic diversity in staff and student body. Approximately 76 percent of all students are Caucasian, 16 percent are Hispanic, and 6 percent are Asian. The remainder of the student body is comprised of African-Americans, Filipinos, American Indian or Alaska Natives, and Pacific Islanders. Combined, over 28 languages are used by students, with about 1,600 students requiring instruction in English as a second language each year.

(top) The Memory Walk charity event benefits Alzheimer's patients by raising money for those in need. Charitable events occur year round in the area and include participants of all ages. Photo by John Eder

(above) Extracurricular activities, clubs, and organizations are essential to a diversified education. Photo courtesy of Agoura High School

(left) The Las Virgenes Unified School District is home to National Blue Ribbon Schools and California Distinguished Schools. Photo courtesy of White Oak Elementary School

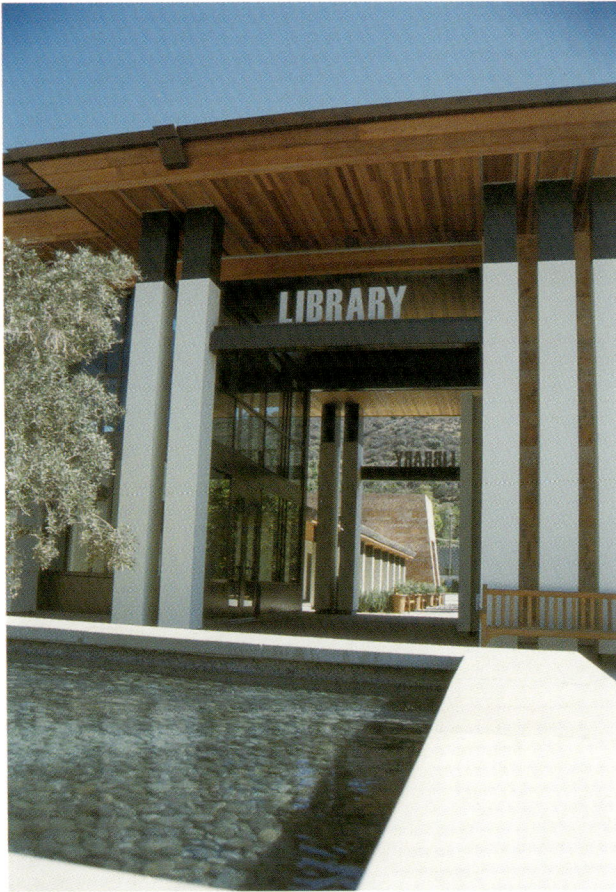

The Westlake Village City Hall and Library are both housed in a unique office park where the design is open and inviting. The library offers the latest in modern technology with its multi-media services and electronics for the public to use. Top photo by John Eder, bottom photo courtesy of the Thousand Oaks-Westlake Village Regional Chamber of Commerce

Local high school students are active in numerous pursuits, including student government, clubs, music programs, and civic duties. Many of the activities and student organizations have won notice and acclaim at the state, regional, and national level. Among the most notable of these endeavors are the mock trial events, sport teams and individual sport competitions, debate teams, math teams, foreign language clubs, and dance clubs.

Although the public school systems obviously offer an excellent education for students, there are also quality private schools in the area that represent a wide range of religious and educational practices.

Adults in the area can take advantage of several schools offering continuing education. Programs include virtually any field of interest.

For higher learning, there is the California Lutheran University (CLU), Ventura County's first four-year university. CLU sits on a picturesque 29 acres and offers 34 majors and 28 minors in its College of Arts and Sciences and schools of Business and Education. Founded in 1959 and rooted in the Evangelical Lutheran tradition of Christian faith, the university encourages critical inquiry in matters of both faith and reason and welcomes students of any religious affiliation.

For seven consecutive years, California Lutheran University has been ranked among the "Top 25" universities in the western United States by *U.S. News & World Report* published by *America's Best Colleges Guide*. In the most recent ranking, CLU placed 17th.

CLU's intercollegiate athletic teams compete in the Southern California Intercollegiate Athletic Conference (SCIAC) and the NCAA, Division III. Men's and women's teams compete in football, baseball, basketball, golf, soccer, tennis, and track and field. Since the

fall of 1991, CLU has won 26 SCIAC championships, averaging more than five per season.

Libraries in the area are well equipped to meet the many needs of students and citizens. The Thousand Oaks Library System consists of the Grant R. Brimhall Library and the Newbury Park Branch. Built in 1982 at a cost of $9 million, the $4.9-million yearly operating costs of the main library come from a $42 assessment per household—two times the national average spent on libraries.

The Library System serves 2,000 people each day with 1.2 million items (books, CDs, videos, etc.) checked out annually making the system one of the highest volume libraries nationwide.

The City of Westlake Village built a new 10,000-square-foot library as part of its $8.7-million civic center complex. The Daniel K. Ludwig Library provides Internet service with full text periodicals, CD ROM, and in-depth selection tools, as well as over 50,600 volumes of texts, videos, and audio-recordings on a wide array of topics suited for adult and child entertainment and education. In addition to the library, the Civic Center houses an 11,000-square-foot city hall, a 94-seat council chamber, and a 1,500-square-foot community meeting room. Designed as a contemporary hacienda,

In addition to first-rate schools, multiple libraries such as the area's Grant R. Brimhall Library in Thousand Oaks, provide supplemental education to students of all ages. Whether it is required reading for a class or looking for a novel to read for pleasure, these resources are well equipped to meet many needs. Photo by John Eder

the beautiful new building merges seamlessly with the area's dramatic topography.

The Thousand Oaks-Westlake Village community takes pride in its educational institutions and resources, and the public's support shows in student performances and school spirit. Safety, an important issue to all Americans, is an added plus to attending any of the schools in Thousand Oaks-Westlake Village.

COVENANT HOUSE

UNITED METHODIST CHURCH
OF WESTLAKE VILLAGE

CHURCH SERVICES   8:00, 9:00 & 10:30 am

The United Methodist Church of Westlake Village is one of many religious institutions offering regular worship services and fellowship events. The area is home to over 100 places of worship.
Photo by John Eder

Mr. Clint

The truth itself is not believed
From one who often has deceived

CHAPTER FIVE

5

Let Us Entertain You

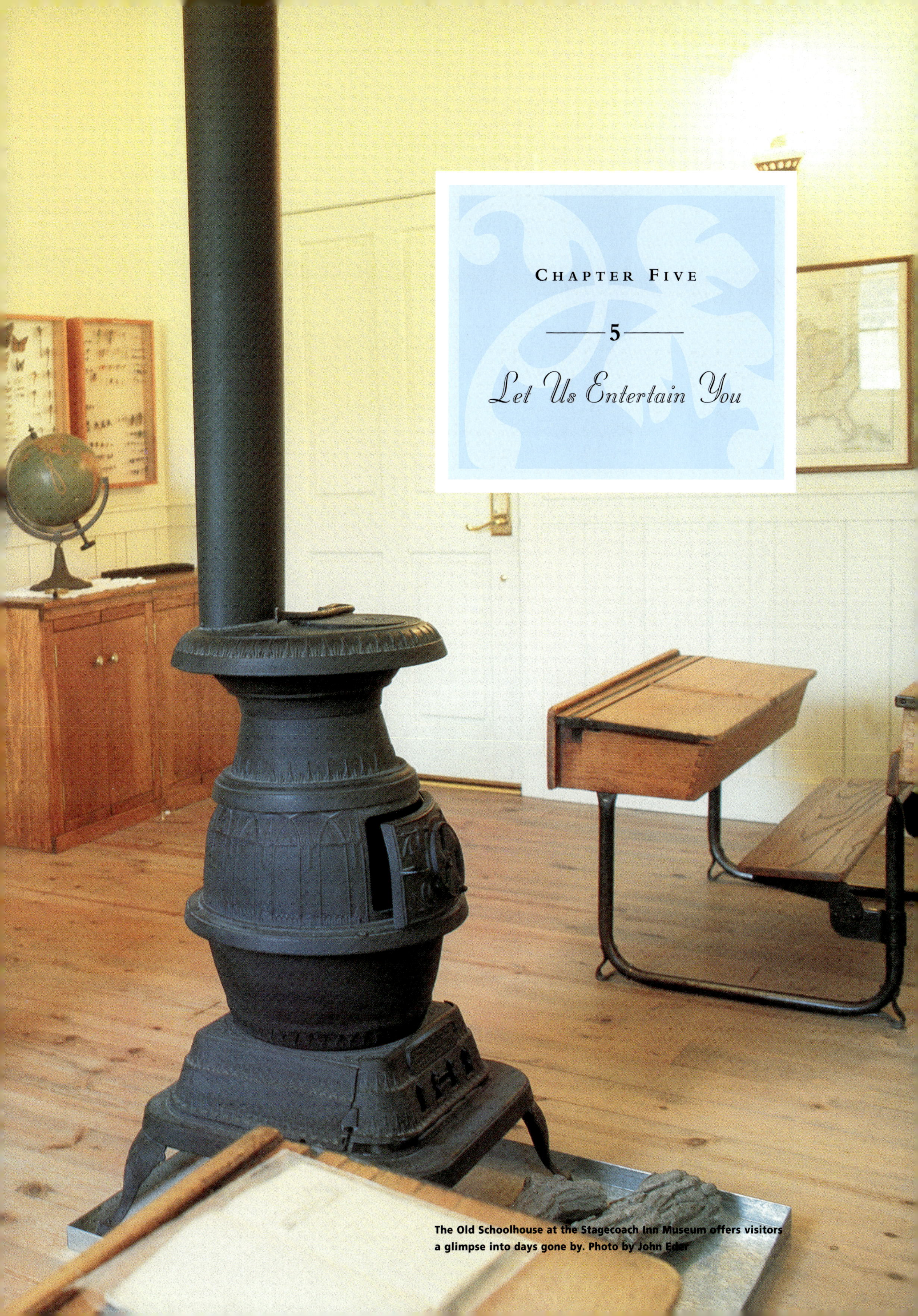

The Old Schoolhouse at the Stagecoach Inn Museum offers visitors a glimpse into days gone by. Photo by John Eder

Human expression not only forms a society but also civilizes it. And, that expression in the form of writings, paintings, sculptures, dance, and music is a strong voice in the Thousand Oaks-Westlake Village area. Both cities offer diversity in cultural and artistic expression, and both have cultural foundations dedicated to the arts.

Thousand Oaks Civic Arts Plaza hosts a wide variety of events from national touring presentations and Broadway musicals to contemporary entertainers of nearly every genre imaginable. Over 2 million people have enjoyed shows like *Cats*, *Les Miserables*, *Rent*, and *A Chorus Line* and such top entertainers as Liza Minnelli, Bill Cosby, David Copperfield, BB King, Sheryl Crow, and Mikhail Baryshnikov at the Thousand Oaks Civic Arts Plaza. Symphony concerts in the 1800-seat Fred Kavli Theatre for the Performing Arts, and concerts and dance recitals in the 400-seat Janet and Ray Scherr Forum Theatre delight audiences throughout the year.

City Hall is also in the Thousand Oaks Civic Arts Plaza complex. Planning Commission and City Council meetings are held in the Janet and Ray Scherr Forum, where 120 of the 400 seats can be lowered to the basement with a flip of a switch to make room for the proceedings.

The 210,000-square-foot Thousand Oats Civic Arts Plaza, ornamented with Indian sandstone, is in itself a work of art. At its highest point, the building towers 10 stories in the air; at its lowest, 22 feet under ground where it is anchored in volcanic rock.

The main stairway from the auditorium to the balcony—the Janss Steps—is an optical illusion. It is built narrower at the top to create

(above) Flowers bloom in abundant profusion at the Gardens of the World. Anyone would become a nature lover viewing this living monument to five cultures. Photo by John Eder

(left) While visiting and touring the Thousand Oaks-Westlake Village area, the Westlake Village Inn is the perfect place to stay. The area is also home to several other reputable hotels offering various amenities like the Hyatt Westlake Plaza Hotel. Photo by John Eder

the impression of a much larger staircase than its actual 68 steps. The lobby doubles as a fine arts gallery for exhibitions by both internationally touring and local artists.

Outside, across from the Thousand Oaks Civic Arts Plaza, is the Gardens of the World, an internationally inspired community park on Thousand Oaks Boulevard.

The Gardens of the World were founded by Ed and Lynn Hogan. They decided to build a striking, living monument to commemorate the various cultures of the world. They wanted to share some of the beauty they had found throughout their world travels. Essentially, the Gardens are divided into five sections: the Japanese Garden, the French Garden and Water Feature, the Mission Courtyard, the English Perennial and Rose Gardens, and the Italian Garden.

The Japanese Garden surrounds an authentic Japanese Pagoda complete with a koi pond, bamboo shoots, and Japanese designed bridges. In the adjacent French Garden, a magnificent, cascading

Thousand Oaks Civic Arts Plaza contains City Hall and a fine arts gallery, and plays host to events such as musicals, entertainers, symphonies, and dance recitals. Photo by John Eder

waterfall is the centerpiece. Flowers and low hedges arranged in intricate designs surround the foot of the waterfall. Colorful hand-painted murals and a Spanish fountain surrounded by olive and citrus trees serve as the focal point in the Mission Courtyard. Nearby in the English Perennial and Rose Gardens, the vibrant, breathtaking colors of the flowers themselves are the sole focus. Completing the international flavor of the Gardens, a romantic grape arbor entwined with lush cabernet and chardonnay grapes surrounded by cypress trees recreates the famed gardens of Italy. A replica of a Victorian bandstand provides a stage for concerts in the park that can be enjoyed from the grassy amphitheater beyond. All of this and more sits just beyond the iron entry gates on the heart of the Boulevard.

Numerous music groups perform regularly throughout the area. The New West Symphony, Conejo Valley Symphony Orchestra, Los Robles Master Chorale, and Village Voices are all popular. The Gold Coast Theatre Conservatory offers classes and opportunities for children to perform in The Conejo Valley Children's Concert Series.

Free concerts in the park in both Thousand Oaks and Westlake Village during summer months feature popular entertainers.

Visual arts are displayed throughout the year in numerous exhibitions, festivals, and shows in a variety of private and public venues. Public exhibits are sponsored by the Conejo Recreation and Park District, Conejo Valley Art Museum, various Rotary Clubs, Thousand Oaks Library, and other community organizations. Several internationally prominent artists have studios in the Conejo Valley.

Other local theatres flourish in the area. The Conejo Players Theater and the Backlot Theater offer a variety of shows throughout the year as do a number of local literary arts groups. Poetry readings, book discussions, writers' conferences, living history tours, speakers' forums, and other related educational events are regularly scheduled at a variety of locations.

The annual Conejo Valley Days celebration attracts residents and visitors from throughout the region. The festivities celebrate the Conejo's colorful past with parades, a chili cook-off, a grand marshall's race, a "Whiskeroo" contest, a carnival, and main-stage entertainers. There is also a two-day rodeo featuring professional cowboys competing for coveted points to qualify for the annual National Rodeo Finals. Top competitors buck their way to the top

Exterior view of the Thousand Oaks Civic Arts Plaza at night. Photo courtesy of the Thousand Oaks Civic Arts Plaza

as a fitting part of celebrating Conejo Valley Days. Bull riding, steer wrestling, calf roping, barrel racing, and bareback riding are among the events.

The Stagecoach Inn Museum Complex also revels in the past. One of the first American-built structures in the area, the Stagecoach Inn houses and demonstrates life in the Wild West. Anderson Hall, on the lower level of the museum, contains fossils and Chumash artifacts, as well as rock and mineral exhibits and a butterfly collection. The Carriage House is the repository for coaches, horse tack, antique tools, and Remington Stagecoach prints. A 1930 Model A Ford is parked nearby. Other structures on the grounds

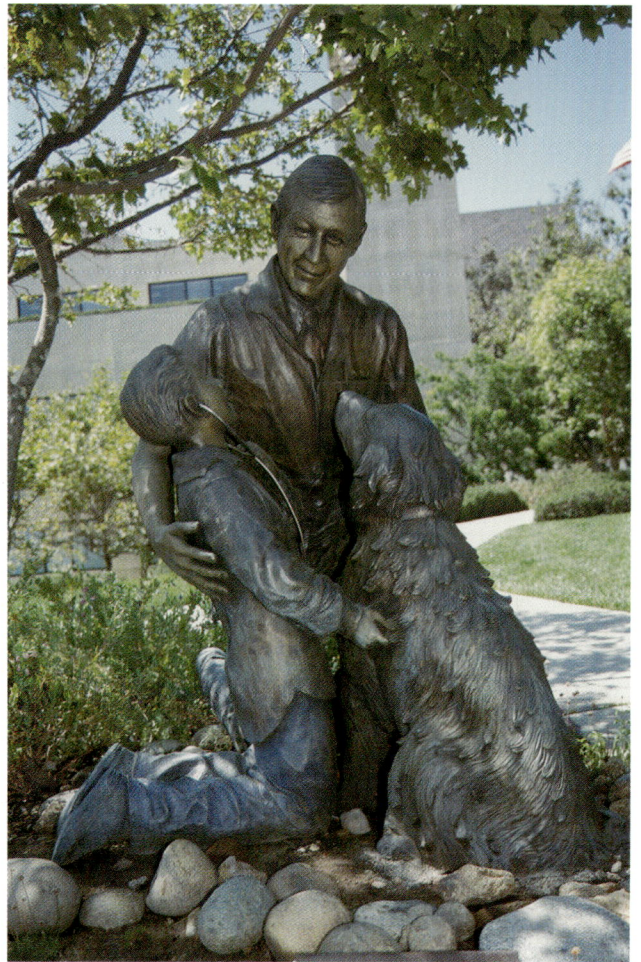

(above) The New West Symphony, one of numerous music groups performing in the area, offers locals a chance to experience music in an elegant setting. Photo by Bill Appleton

(right) The Thousand Oaks Civic Arts Plaza is beautifully decorated inside with fine art, and outside with magnificent sculptures. Photo by John Eder

depict life in the early days, including a windmill, a blacksmith shop, and a beehive oven.

Three houses from different time periods are also on the museum grounds. The Pioneer or Newbury House is a replica of Egbert Starr Newbury's (the area's first postmaster) home, built in 1874. The Adobe House is similar to homes occupied by early Mexican settlers, and the Chumash Hut, built with bulrushes and designed to house 30 Indians, is identical to those used by the Native Americans for at least 3,000 years.

Completing the museum complex are a huge Sycamore tree, designated as a Ventura County landmark because of its age, size, and formation; a rose garden; and a nature trail.

Other local or nearby historic sites of interest include Independence Square in Westlake Village, the Chumash Interpretive Center in Thousand Oaks, and the Ronald Reagan Presidential Library and Museum in Simi Valley.

It is clear that Thousand Oaks and Westlake Village offer a wide variety of things to do from the purely educational to the wildly entertaining, with wonderful facilities that do both. New entertainment opportunities are being planned for the near future. ❧

© Disney

(top) Disney's *Beauty and the Beast* took place in the Fred Kavli Theatre in September 2002. Photo courtesy of Theatre League

(above) A community performance in the Janet and Ray Scherr Forum. Photo courtesy of the Thousand Oaks Civic Arts Plaza

(left) Even the hallways in the Thousand Oaks Civic Arts Plaza are unique and create an unusual ambiance. It is also home to a staircase that creates an optical illusion with the top being narrower, giving the impression that it is much larger. Photo by John Eder

Thousand Oaks is proud to be the home of the Gardens of the World. It sprawls over 4.5 acres and includes a fitness trail, amphitheater for performances, and many mission gardens. Photo by John Eder

Chapter Six

6

The Sporting Life

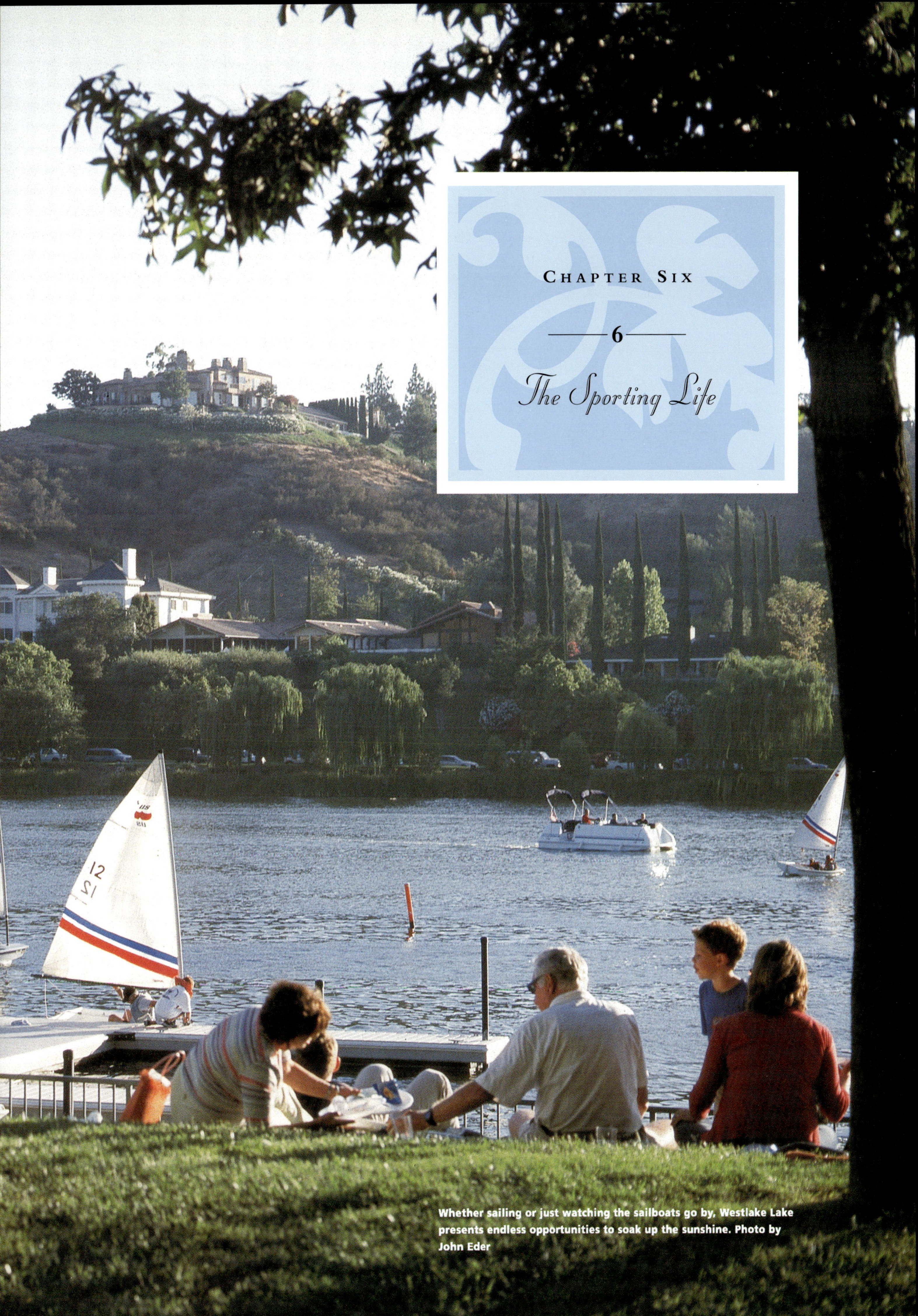

Whether sailing or just watching the sailboats go by, Westlake Lake presents endless opportunities to soak up the sunshine. Photo by John Eder

ℛecreation is restorative for hard-working souls of any age. There is no limit to the range of recreational opportunities and sites in the Greater Los Angeles-Ventura area where seashore and mountains, lakes and deserts, cities and farms, natural wildlife, and working ranches are all compacted within a 165-mile radius.

And with every type of terrain imaginable comes every type of sport under the sun!

Adjacent to Westlake Village, the Santa Monica Mountains National Recreation Area's abundant nature trails provide varying levels of difficulty for both experienced and inexperienced hikers, backpackers, mountain bikers, picnickers, equestrians, and campers. Naturalist classes, Indian arts and handicrafts, art exhibits, concerts, and other activities are regularly scheduled on site as well. Despite its massive array of nature experiences, the Santa Monica Mountains National Recreation Area is just the beginning of the area's outdoor opportunities.

The "Big Sycamore to the Sea" is a relatively easy eight-mile hike or mountain bike ride from Rancho Sierra Vista in Newbury Park to the ocean via Point Mugu State Park. Indian Creek Trail to Paradise Falls in Wildwood Regional Park in Thousand Oaks is an easy to moderate hike through a shady canyon to an 80-foot water-fall. The trail is two miles round trip.

The Conejo Recreation and Park District in Thousand Oaks manages 33 developed parks, five playfield parks, one district-wide

park, and the 1300-acre Wildwood Park, plus 12,000 acres of open space and 75 miles of nature trails. The District offers more than 2,500 organized recreation and leisure programs every year. Westlake Village offers three city parks and a recreation program with organized sports for youth in soccer, football, softball, baseball, basketball, swimming, boating, and track and field.

Thousand Oaks and Westlake Village are literally covered with scenic sidewalks, green belts, and protected bike lanes. Several neighborhoods have equestrian trail networks. Places to walk, jog, hike, ride horses, golf, and play tennis abound.

Residents enjoy boating and fishing at the privately owned Westlake's 150-acre lake which is regularly stocked with fresh-water fish including bass, blue gill, and catfish. Commercial harbors nearby offer saltwater sports fishing and whale watching tours.

Golf is another favored pastime in the area. Private courses include North Ranch Country Club in Westlake Village and Sherwood Country Club and Sunset Hills Country Club, both in Thousand Oaks. Public courses include Westlake Village Golf Course and Los Robles Greens in Thousand Oaks.

Numerous tennis court locations and several public swimming pools add to the outdoor recreational choices. In Thousand Oaks, the Conejo Recreation District maintains public tennis courts at the Thousand Oaks Community Center, Wildflower Park, North Ranch Park, and Borchard Community Center in Newbury Park.

Other tennis courts open to the public are available at California Lutheran University and Thousand Oaks High School. Thousand Oaks and Westlake Village also boast a variety of private tennis clubs to choose from.

For a break from the sun, the local teen center provides numerous programs for kids ages 12 to 17 that include indoor sports, music and dance, arts, health and safety, and a wide variety of social activities. The Alex Fiore Thousand Oaks Teen Center serves 250-350 teenagers a day and hosts concerts, monthly dances, rollerblade contests, sports league competitions, and more. In addition, the YMCA and The Boys and Girls Clubs are also coming to the area soon by renovating existing locations and building new locations. Both communities are very supportive of youth sports and contract with the Conejo Recreation and Park District to provide services.

The Goebel Senior Adult Center for people over 55 years old offers a filled calendar of activities and events that start early in the morning and run through late evening every day of the year. Approximately 11,000 seniors are served monthly with over 106 different weekly programs and eight separate social services. Sample activities include aquatic lessons, zoo trips, bridge games, billiards, painting, dancing, memoir writing classes, league bowling, classes of every description, sightseeing tours, field trips, and a bonanza of volunteer opportunities.

Whether it is a bike ride or a membership to a local gym, residents in the Conejo Valley have abundant recreational opportunities all year long. ꦥ

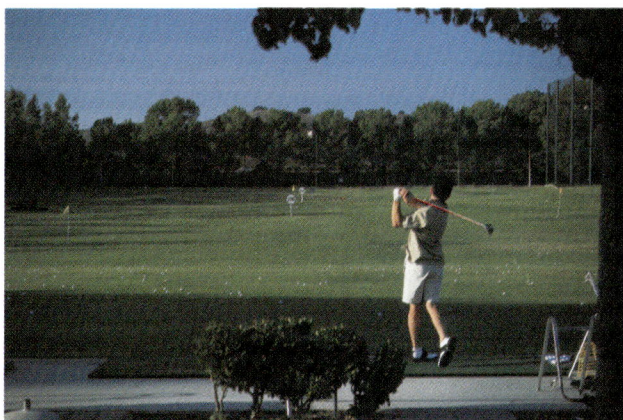

(previous page) The setting of Thousand Oaks and Westlake Village provide a perfect place to horseback ride. The Santa Monica Mountains National Recreation Area provides numerous trails, as do several neighborhoods. Photo by John Eder

(left) The area's temperate climate means golfers can hit the links practically any day of the year. Photo by John Eder

(bottom) Surfers flock to County Line Beach for sea, surf, and a clean beach. Photo by John Eder

Hikers and bikers enjoy the Santa Monica Mountains National Recreation Area (left and right) while others choose the quiet elegance of Westlake Yacht Club (above). Photos by John Eder

Two frequently overlooked groups, teenagers and the elderly, find fun and companionship at the Goebel Senior Adult Center (left) and Alex Fiore Thousand Oaks Teen Center (above). Photos by John Eder

Golf is a popular sport in the Thousand Oaks-Westlake Village area due to the mild climate and relaxing nature of the sport. There are several public and private courses to appease residents and their guests. Photo by John Eder

Part Two

CHAPTER SEVEN

7

Manufacturing, Distribution & High Technology

Photo by John Eder

DOLE FOOD COMPANY, INC.

A name recognized in many languages in almost every land, Dole Food Company, Inc. is the world's largest producer and marketer of fresh fruit, fresh vegetables, and fresh-cut flowers, and markets a growing line of packaged food. Dole sells over 170 different food products and is the industry's leading producer of canned and fresh pineapple, the largest banana company in the United States and one of the largest in the world, and the premier North American supplier of fresh-cut salads, lettuce, celery, broccoli, and cauliflower.

Today's consumer is looking for nutritious foods that fit a healthy, active lifestyle. Dole meets these needs with fresh, nutritious, wholesome products that offer convenience and great taste with unsurpassed variety. With more than 70 fresh fruits and vegetables, and over 100 processed and packaged fruits and juices, Dole is recognized by 98 percent of American consumers for high-quality, nutritious food products.

To answer growing consumer demand for healthy, easy-to-prepare meals and snacks, Dole continues to introduce tasty new variations in value added products, including fresh-cut salads. Dole is a leader in this industry, which has been the fastest growing category in supermarkets.

Founded in Hawaii in 1851, the company built its reputation on its commitment to "quality, and quality, and quality." These were the words of James Drummond Dole's "Statement of Principles," upon which he founded and operated the company. Dole came to Hawaii with an initial investment of $1,000, degrees in business and horticulture, and a love of farming to begin the first successful pineapple growing and canning operation, then called Hawaiian Pineapple Company. Dole developed and grew the pineapple business into Hawaii's second largest industry. In achieving his goal of making pineapple available in every grocery store in the country, James Dole made the name "Hawaiian" almost synonymous with "pineapple." Considered an

Dole provides a bountiful array of fresh fruit and vegetables to help individuals incorporate five to nine servings of fruits and vegetables per day in their diets. Dole is a founding member of the National 5 A Day for Better Health Program and is a leader in developing technology-based nutrition education programs for children.

exotic fruit, pineapple became the sign of hospitality and is often depicted on fine furniture and in home decor.

Dole's multi-product line is marketed not only in North America, but also throughout the world by the more than 100 Dole sales offices and brokers. This worldwide team of growers, packers, processors, shippers, and employees is committed to consistently providing safe, high quality fruit, vegetables and food products, along with fresh-cut flowers, while protecting the environment in which its products are grown and processed. Jim Dole's dedication to quality is still the top priority. It is a commitment solidly backed by comprehensive programs for food safety, stringent quality control measures, state-of-the-art production and transportation technologies, nutrition education

Moving Dole's millions of cases of products around the world involves an extensive distribution system. Dole has the industry's most modern fleet of refrigerated container vessels to deliver its products, ensuring that the items delivered to the neighborhood grocery store arrive in peak condition.

programs, continuous improvement through research and innovation, scientific pest management programs, and dedication to the safety of its workers, communities, and the environment.

Dole has been recognized for its environmental practices, including being ranked among the top ten companies for environmental and social responsibility as well as receiving the Ethical Workplace Award. Dole leads the industry in the environmental area with virtually all its farming facilities worldwide certified to the highest environmental management practices by internationally recognized accrediting organizations.

Dole has long been a major sponsor of local sports events in order to raise funds for charities. Currently, Dole is a major sponsor of the Target World Challenge, a golf tournament held annually at picturesque Sherwood Country Club, situated just a few miles from Dole's worldwide headquarters in Westlake Village, California. The event is hosted by PGA superstar Tiger Woods and brings together a select field of 20 of golf's top professionals. Since it began in 2000, the tournament and its sponsors have helped raise millions of dollars for children's charities.

The company also participates in community based events by donating funds or products to health oriented programs. The goal of its charitable contribution program is to help effect positive change particularly in the area of nutrition education for children as a way to prevent disease. Dole is also one of the largest donors to nationwide feeding programs.

For years, Dole has been a leader in nutrition education for children, working in collaboration with many of the nation's leading health authorities to teach students the value of healthy eating habits. The company created the first non-branded CD-ROM

A thing of beauty—the DOLE® banana signifies high quality and nutritious fruit grown in an environmentally responsible manner. One Dole banana provides 16 percent of the fiber, 15 percent of the Vitamin C, and 11 percent of the potassium needed every day for good health.

Consumers select from over 170 DOLE® products from nearly every aisle of the supermarket. Dole's Healthy Foods Center provides valuable information on the nutritional content of DOLE® products, helpful tips for their selection and storage, and many healthful and mouthwatering recipes.

program designed especially to educate elementary grade students about the benefits of proper nutrition. Bobby Banana®, Pinellopy Pineapple, Anthony Apple, and Sammy Salad come to life with individual personalities and voices through interactive multimedia and discovery learning in a way that excites children about nutrition. Dole has donated this non-branded program to over 34,000 schools and over 100,000 teachers nationwide. Dole also developed a nutrition education web site that is available on the Internet at www.dole5aday.com.

As part of Dole's ongoing effort to promote healthy, nutritious foods and lifestyles, the company, along with medical and nutrition experts from The Mayo Clinic and University of California at Los Angeles (UCLA), prepared *The Encyclopedia of Foods: A Guide to Healthy Nutrition*, a beautifully photographed and illustrated 500-page resource on what to eat for maximum health. The book is available to order on-line on the www.dole.com website.

Innovative ideas, along with a relentless commitment to providing high-quality products, are the keys to success at Dole Food Company. Dole and its nearly 60,000 employees are dedicated to these principles. The company's worldwide team takes pride in building the Dole brand and maintaining the premium market position of its products.

VIVITAR CORPORATION

In the late 1930s, Hollywood was firmly entrenched in its Golden Era and Los Angeles was beginning to come of age. The nation was emerging from World War I and the economy was beginning its transition to a more stable pattern. The city of Los Angeles was a magnet for innovation, invention, and creativity, attracting the eyes of two German immigrants, Max Ponder and John Best who decided to capitalize on an emerging industry—amateur and consumer photography. The two men made the decision to form a company in 1938 and named it Ponder & Best after themselves.

Ponder & Best served an integral role in the transition to post-war times. Utilizing 1,200 highly skilled employees, the company begat an extensive design and manufacturing facility that manufactured lenses as well as photographic accessories. In 1977, the company changed its name and the Vivitar Corporation was born.

Today, this highly consumer-accepted brand name company is headquartered in Newbury Park and designs, develops, and markets photographic, optical, electronic, and digital imaging products through offices across the globe in such locales as France, Hong Kong, the United Kingdom, and the United States. Vivitar's line of imaging products are family-oriented and are kept at prices within the reach of families and advanced amateurs, yet still are able to provide an exceptional value to consumers with few Vivitar products priced over $499. Yet, the corporation also manufactures an outstanding line of lenses and flash units to appeal to the needs of the demanding professional photographer, creating a benchmark of excellence within the photographic industry.

Consistently ranked in the top-five of camera (and camera accessories) suppliers in the United States, Vivitar has compiled an impressive list of patents and technological innovations that have set many standards in the photographic industry. The Vivitar portfolio contains over 85 electronic flash and optics patents, which have spurred many photographic manufacturers worldwide to incorporate into each of their own flash and 35 mm SLR zoom lenses. In recent

Gary Carleton-President, CEO.

years, the corporation has accumulated several awards for product innovation from the Photographic Marketing Association and the Digital Imaging Marketing Association.

Vivitar has always played an important role in the community ever since its days as Ponder & Best, contributing significantly to the economic development and maturation of Los Angeles. After spending several decades in West Los Angeles, Vivitar relocated to the San Fernando Valley as Los Angeles continued to grow and expand. Vivitar's facilities were destroyed in the Northridge earthquake of 1994 and relocated to the Conejo Valley in what would soon become known as the 101 tech corridor. Just as it had done in 1938, Vivitar once again participated in a significant trend in the economic growth and development of the area.

The world of photography has endured many changes over the years with many of those changes occurring in recent decades with technology advancing in rapid fashion. While the current trend is moving rapidly towards digital imaging, the large filmmakers are at a cross road. Photo processing is being redefined in the digital age and processors are witnessing a gradual but steady decline in their business. Whereas Vivitar is neither a filmmaker nor a film-processor, it is heavily influenced by the trends and changes in the photographic industry.

Vivitar Corporation Board of Directors: (left to right) Gary Carleton, President/CEO; Cliff Montgomery, Vice President Sales/Marketing; Vic Chernick, Chairman of the Board; and Fumio Hayashi, Vice President/General Manager.

But with all of the changes that technology has provided the industry, one fact remains the same: people still like to take images and share them with others. Still-images (as opposed to video) continues to be the predominant means by which people record and capture the memories and moments of their life. Imaging still remains one of the more significant popular hobbies and serve as the universal language throughout the world.

The transition to digital has been a revolutionary change in the photo industry. To date, digital imaging is not a mature industry with only the filmmakers and major Japanese brands, with their enormous cash-generating film and camera businesses could afford to sustain the heavy investment and operating losses that are associated with digital. The transition from silver-based imaging to digital has been one of the major challenges for these established brands. More flexible players like Vivitar that manufacture in partner factories are uniquely positioned and competitively postured for future imaging products characterized by shorter development cycles, limited product life-cycles, and shorter margins.

By design, Vivitar is substantially smaller than its competitors in the industry, operating with lower overhead, a smaller infrastructure, and less management bureaucracy than its peers. Because of this, Vivitar is able to adjust and change quicker than others in the industry, which has had a positive lasting impact on the company itself as well as the industry as a whole.

(above) Vivitar DP-1500X Digital Projector.

(below) Series 1 Lenses.

With a seasoned management team, competitive cost-structure, partner-manufacturers, and a compelling product line, Vivitar is well positioned to continue its growth as a competitive player in the digital imaging industry. ✿

HANSON LAB FURNITURE

*E*stablished in 1977, Hanson Lab Furniture is a full service steel laboratory furniture design, manufacturer, and installer of metal laboratory casework and fume hoods. By specializing in lab planning and metal laboratory furniture, Hanson Lab Furniture is able to supply the highest quality project design and installation of steel casework laboratories.

Serving the laboratory furniture needs of the scientific community, Hanson Lab Furniture is currently under the guidance of Mike Hanson, President and CEO and Joseph Matta, V.P. Business Development. Combined, the duo's industry expertise and commitment to providing personalized service far beyond the industry standards has set the tone for all Hanson Lab Furniture customer relations.

Ideally situated in the Conejo Valley, Hanson Lab Furniture is the only manufacturer of metal lab furniture and fume hoods on the west coast. By remaining in close proximity to its customers, the company is able to avoid needless delays and added expenses that are

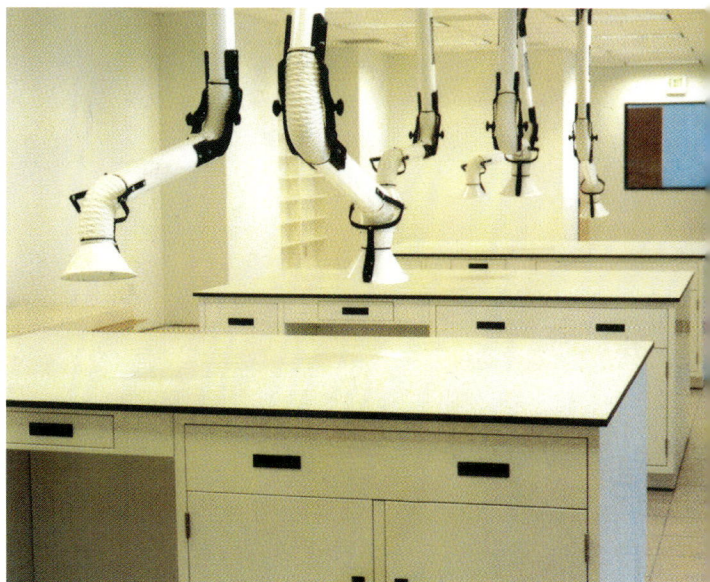

Laboratory work stations.

oftentimes caused by shipping such heavy product over long distances. Its physical location has assisted in helping Hanson Lab Furniture remain true to its corporate mission statement's goal of providing the highest quality of product with the quickest response time to the purchasers of laboratory furniture.

The staff at Hanson Lab Furniture takes great pride in its customer relations and strives to provide each client with the utmost in care and respect. The thoroughly trained Lab Planning Specialists meet with each client and discusses the client's needs and dreams. Information is gathered to the smallest details before returning in a matter of days with concept drawings and estimates to insure that the customer is aware of every stage of the operation. By turning the needs, concerns, safety requirements, and concepts of the client into details, solutions, designs, and a laboratory that fits every one of their needs, Hanson Lab Furniture takes the extra step in making the process as informative yet comprehensive as possible.

All of the energies at Hanson Lab Furniture remain focused exclusively on planning, manufacturing, and installing the client's laboratory furniture. The organization brings a depth of knowledge that remains rare in the industry. Hanson Lab Furniture works closely with the architects, electricians, and other workers, helping to coordinate the entire project to ensure that it all runs smoothly. This same dedication in service is given to each client whether they need a small lab remodeled or are building multiple laboratories. Because at Hanson Lab Furniture, the customer's satisfaction depends on the company's careful attention to each and every detail no matter how big or small. 🐾

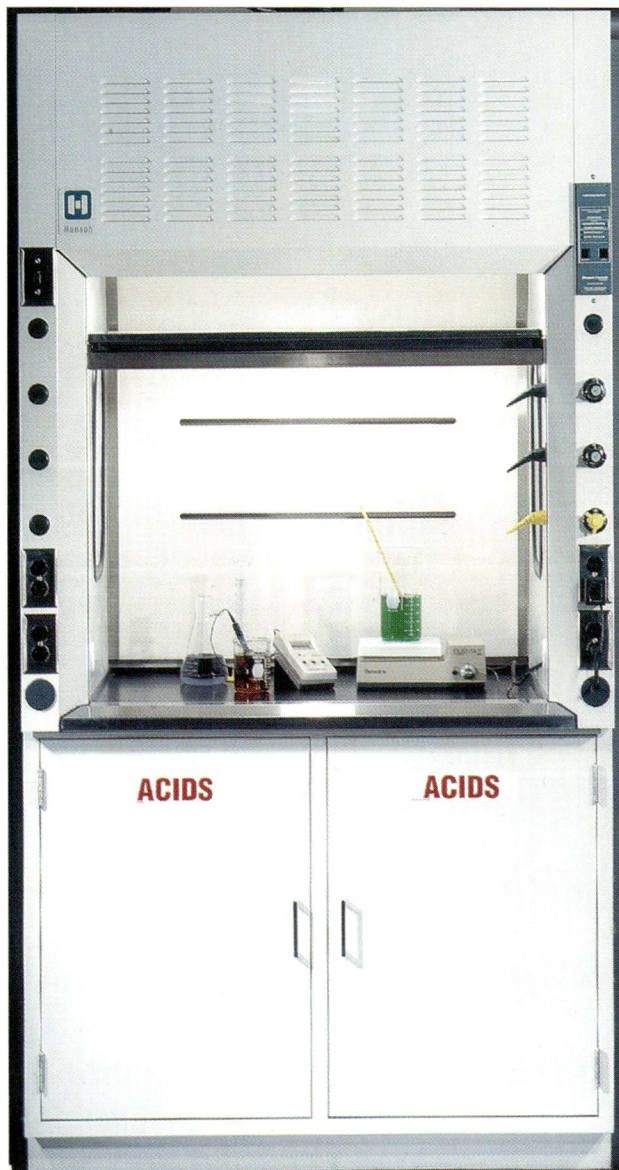

Benchtop fumehood with chemical storage.

MARKET SCAN INFORMATION SYSTEMS, INC.

*I*n the past, automobile dealerships required a great deal of manpower and long hours in order to research and find the best financing options for each of their customers. Thanks to the products and services developed by Market Scan Information Systems, Inc., those days are long forgotten.

Market Scan has kept automobile dealerships on the cutting edge since 1988. When Russell and Rusty West first began entertaining the idea of creating the company, they had one mission in mind: To develop a fast, accurate, and easy-to-use system that would assist dealerships in providing their customers with the best financing options available in the market for every potential deal—regardless of the customer's credit or negative equity challenges—while helping them meet their profit objectives.

Market Scan's first solution was named Lease Prophet®. This software package featured the most comprehensive database of new car lease programs in the world and it could find the scientifically perfect lease program in a matter of seconds. It quickly became the standard by which all lease finance systems were measured. In the years since Lease Prophet was first released, several new products have been introduced, including Lease Prophet for Used Vehicles and the Retail Finance System for traditional purchase transactions. Early last year, the Dealership Management System (DMS) Integration package was introduced, allowing dealerships to download their entire inventory so that sales managers could quickly and easily scan for the ideal vehicles to suit each customer's needs in just a matter of minutes. At the same time, Market Scan developed a Networked Version, which makes sharing information at multiple desks within the same dealership much easier. In 2002, the Market Scan database housed over 190,000 retail finance and lease programs, maintaining its position as the industry leader. Most recently, the company introduced its Quik Sales Kiosk™, a state-of-the-art customer entry point for auto dealerships, allowing the dealers to present deal information and options to customers quicker than ever to improve customer service and satisfaction.

To date, there have been more than 5,000 Market Scan systems installed across the nation. In California alone, Market Scan's customers deliver more than 83 percent of all showroom leases—over $6 billion annually. Today, small dealerships and large dealer groups alike, find the Market Scan system instrumental to their growth and profitability. Clients include the largest and most successful dealer groups in the world. With offices and training centers in Los Angeles, New York, Cincinnati, and Tampa, Market Scan is equipped to provide dealerships with excellent service—and a remarkably enhanced bottom line.

The vision, experience, and resources that Market Scan makes available to its customers ensures they will consistently dominate their respective markets and stay firmly on the cutting edge of the industry.

(top) Market Scan Information Systems, Inc. Employees at Westlake Village Headquarters.

(above) Market Scan's Chief Executive Officer, Rusty West, and Liaison Department Manager, Sabrina Hayes, with the company's latest innovation, the *Quik Sales Kiosk*™.

Photo by John Eder

THE THOUSAND OAKS-WESTLAKE VILLAGE REGIONAL CHAMBER OF COMMERCE

The Chamber acts as the voice for the business community. In business, a single voice can often go unheard, while the collective, united voice of the Chamber has often proven effective and beneficial to business. There are challenges and opportunities which individuals themselves cannot solve or reach. By working with others and pooling time and resources, however, important accomplishments are made.

For many years in the Conejo Valley there were two Chambers of Commerce operating separately: The Conejo Valley Chamber in Thousand Oaks and the Westlake Village Chamber. While each Chamber had its fair share of members, the respective Boards of Directors also realized that the strength of the individual organizations emanated from its members and, therefore, merged the two organizations. The merger of these two strong chambers created what is now the Thousand Oaks Westlake Village Regional Chamber of Commerce. This organization formed a membership base that empowered them to increase benefits and services, and create a stronger more influential presence in the Conejo Valley.

The Thousand Oaks-Westlake Village Regional Chamber of Commerce is a member-driven, professionally staffed non-profit organization dedicated to supporting the region's business community. This Chamber is unique in that they represent two separate cities that cross over two county lines. Listing more than 1,600 business and professional firms as members, the organization has solidified its standing as one of the state's largest Chambers of Commerce. These 1,600 members serve as the backbone of the organization, forming a pool of resources from which ideas, manpower, and support are nurtured. After all, a rich diversity of business provides a strong and stable economic foundation.

Membership in the Chamber provides advantages designed to meet business needs in areas such as business promotion, advertising and publicity, education, and legislative representation. The

Ribbon cutting ceremonies.

organization also serves as an excellent source for networking, and giving business owners several opportunities to establish new relationships and contacts with other business owners in the area. Being a member of the Thousand Oaks-Westlake Village Regional Chamber of Commerce has countless advantages and serves as one of the most important investments a business can make.

The Thousand Oaks-Westlake Village Regional Chamber of Commerce is governed by a Board of Directors representing small, medium, and large businesses. Among the large businesses, several of the area's top ten employers are represented; bringing together a talented cross section of the wide variety of business entities in the Conejo Valley. This distinguished group works with the Chamber staff to be a valuable resource to the business community.

The Chamber additionally has an active group of volunteer businesses that represent the welcoming arm of the Chamber. This group is referred to as the Chamber Ambassadors. They are a valuable resource for acclimating our newest members as well as guiding our existing members. Together, the Board of Directors, staff, and Ambassadors encourage communication with its members and the development of programs and services that address the diverse challenges that members face in this ever-changing world.

The Chamber holds the distinction of being an accredited Chamber, an honor awarded by the U.S. Chamber of Commerce. Only 600 of the more than 6,000 chambers have been awarded this honor. Accredited Chambers must have a proven, sound structure, approved governing bylaws, and have undergone an extensive review of the activities of their Board, staff, and committees. While the accreditation process is arduous, the rewards have proven to be tremendous. Achieving accreditation places this chamber in the top ten percent of chambers in the nation.

The Thousand Oaks-Westlake Village Regional Chamber of Commerce realizes that business is only as strong as the community in which it is located. In that

Chamber committees.

respect, the Chamber maintains an ongoing dialog with local and state policy makers to ensure that business and the community thrives. The Chamber also has a strong commitment to giving back to the community through a myriad of committees and events held throughout the year. The Great Pumpkin Runs, Business Expos, State of the City Luncheons, Economic Outlook Luncheon, the Annual Auto Show, Candidates Forums, and Ribbon Cuttings fill the annual calendar with opportunities for activism, education, and entertainment. Its Human Resources Council, Marketing, Technology, and Government Relations committees provide additional resources for building strong business practices through a variety of seminars and workshops. The Chamber's Education Committee carries out such valuable programs as Teacher of the Month, Principal for 1/2 Day, and scholarships for exceptional high school seniors.

It's no wonder that the Thousand Oaks–Westlake Village Regional Chamber of Commerce carries as its mission statement: "To promote the quality of life in Thousand Oaks and Westlake Village through economic vitality." This organization proves its commitment by offering outstanding economic development, legislative advocacy, and business strengthening opportunities critical to the stability and growth of the area's business climate. In fact, after being named as one of the *Los Angeles Journal*'s picks for the top 25 Chambers, this Chamber received a formal commendation from the Lieutenant Governor of the State of California which stated: "I am delighted to commend you for your enduring commitment to the State of California. I admire your dedication to strengthening the

(top) Business Expo Trade Show.

(above) Great Pumpkin Runs.

economic vitality of the region and welcome your continued efforts to enrich the lives of others. Your leadership sets a wonderful example for all Californians."

Clearly, the Thousand Oaks–Westlake Village Regional Chamber of Commerce plays a key role in bringing together two great cities with an exceptional combination of community, culture, and business. ☙

BEHR BROWERS ARCHITECTS, INC.

ehr Browers Architects, Inc. (BBA) is a specialized but diverse award-winning architectural firm that has become nationally recognized for its innovative cinema designs. In addition to being responsible for the design and planning of over 100 multiplex cinemas across the country, the firm is also renowned for its extensive master planning and urban design experience.

BBA has served as design and renovation architect to major landmark cinemas such as Grauman's Chinese Theatre, the Fox Westwood, and the Bruin. The company has nurtured long-term relationships with such theatre clients as Mann Theatres, Brenden Theatres, United Artists, Maya Theatres, and Galaxy Theatres and worked in conjunction with Edwards Cinemas on various projects. Behr Browers Architects has earned its reputation as an expert in buildings requiring special technologies for multimedia presentations and those facilities requiring unique sound control specifications, as well as those requiring historical restoration knowledge.

One of the largest architectural firms in the county, Behr Browers Architects, Inc. was formed in 1987 when founders Francisco Behr, AIA, and Michael Browers, AIA, recognized that their individual talents and experience were complimentary when combined together. They developed these talents and experience into the foundation for what has become a strong architectural practice that is highly respected and admired amongst its peers.

The firm has garnered over a dozen local and national awards for projects such as Mount Sinai Memorial Park in Simi Valley, the Criterion Restoration in Santa Monica, Brenden Theatres in Modesto, Grauman's Chinese Restoration, and the new Chinese 6 in Hollywood.

Founding Principals Michael Browers, Vice President and Francisco Behr, President.

The principals have diverse talents and interests. Francisco Behr has taught design at U.C.L.A.'s Extension Program for 18 years. Mr Behr is an award-winning and nationally recognized urban design consultant, participating in over two dozen workshops throughout the United States. A partial list of those workshops include the Los Angeles General Plan Framework workshops, Kingman, Arizona Chamber of Commerce project, West Hollywood and Sunset Boulevard Specific Plans, Penn Yard, and New York Trump's Television City Workshop. Mr. Behr has traveled extensively throughout the world, drawing inspiration for the firm's high quality designs. His wife, Rossana Behr, is in charge of the financial and personnel portion of the business by serving as the firm's Business Manager and Human Resources Director.

Michael Browers brings 26 years of experience to the firm in a wide range of projects including government and institutional facilities, medical complexes, general offices, local and regional malls and shopping centers, and corporate headquarters buildings. In addition, he has over 15 years experience in the design of state-of-the-art movie theatres and related entertainment facilities, as well as extensive experience dealing with community groups, special committees, and regulatory organizations.

Locally, the firm has been responsible for the design of several of the largest and most complex master plans in the community. Master plans for the Seventh-day Adventist Schools, the Dos Vientos Town Center, and Richland Communities' half-million square-foot office complex in Westlake Village have all been created by Behr Browers Architects. Outside of the Conejo Valley, the Firm was responsible for the preparation of a transit-planning document for downtown Los Angeles and the preparation of an urban design strategic plan for the City of Bell Garden's commercial corridor.

This interior view of the Mount Sinai chapel shows the interplay of stone, wood, and natural lighting to create a warm and comforting space in this high-quality memorial facility. Behr Browers Architects' experience with institutional projects also includes churches, schools, senior care facilities, libraries, and governmental facilities.

Behr Browers Architects, Inc. has also designed several landmark and public benefit projects in the community. In addition to several local movie theatres, the firm has designed two buildings for Amgen, the Newbury Park Branch Library, Senior Concerns' original Fitzgerald House building and expansion, as well as several retail centers.

Both Mr. Behr and Mr. Browers have been active citizens in the affairs of the region, donating their time and expertise to a number of projects and non-profit organizations, including the Conejo Valley Chamber of Commerce, the Alliance for the Arts, the Gold Coast Association, Thousand Oaks Boulevard Association, HOME, and the Boys & Girls Club to name a few. Behr Browers Architects also continues to be strong advocates of affordable housing, mixed-use zoning, innovative planning, fair treatment of the development community, smart growth, green design, and environmental preservation.

Andrew Althaus, Senior Associate, together with the knowledgeable and talented staff are not limited to just traditional architectural problems as is demonstrated by its winning a national design competition for the conceptual design of a new transit vehicle. This creative team is committed to designs that are not only functional but also exceptionally beautiful.

The firm is as concerned about their clients' overall image and brand as they are about the buildings and has assisted many of its clients in developing corporate and brand identity images and materials. Overall, the firm's sensitivity to the constraints and budgets of the various projects allows it to provide facilities and designs that meet—and often times exceed—client expectations.

The world-renown Grauman's Chinese Theatre underwent a state-of-the-art technological upgrade, historical restoration, and seismic retrofit under the direction of Behr Browers Architects.

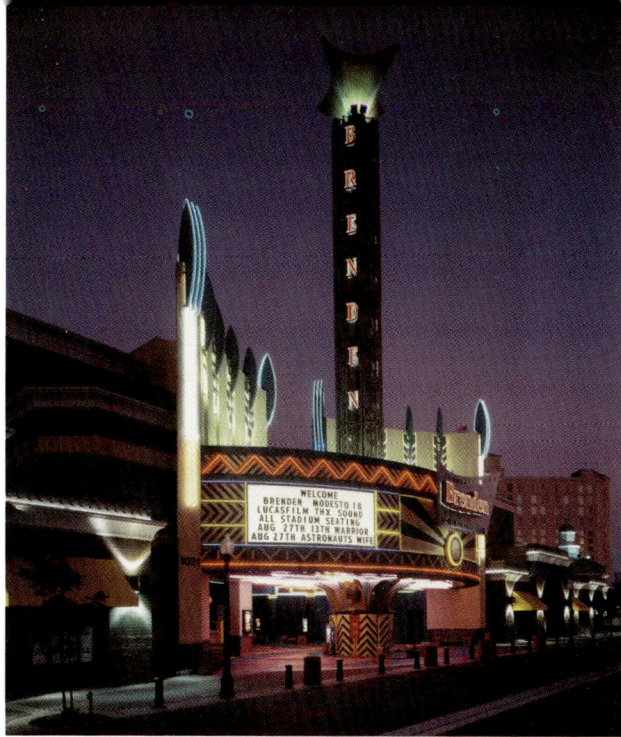

As part of an award-winning revitalization effort in Modesto, Behr Browers Architects designed this stadium movie theatre to be reminiscent of historical downtown movie theatres. Behr Browers Architects is recognized for their movie theatre expertise throughout the United States.

Having mastered the art of creating exciting and new concepts for theatres, retail, and entertainment facilities, Behr Browers Architects, Inc. is slowly expanding its expertise to include several specialized services and skills for projects such as educational facilities, high tech office parks and mixed-use centers. In addition, the firm is initiating services in conceptual landscape design, furniture design, including selection and purchase, and graphic design.

However, at the core of the firm's services lie the main goal of continuing to provide quality services that will in turn positively enhance every community, every building and every object that it is commissioned in an effective, efficient, and artistic manner.

J.D. POWER AND ASSOCIATES

*V*ery few marketing information firms have had such a positive impact in the business world as J.D. Power and Associates. The firm's quality and customer satisfaction research has been instrumental in helping industries focus on and improve product quality and satisfaction. Established in 1968 by J.D. Power III, the firm conducts independent and unbiased surveys of customer satisfaction, product quality, and buyer behavior.

Each year, the firm surveys millions of consumers and business customers to gauge their satisfaction with the products and services they purchase. J.D. Power and Associates is a privately held organization that funds its own studies. In doing so, the firm's study results are not influenced by the industries it serves.

A pioneer in the field of consumer-based marketing research for more than 40 years, Mr. Power's lifelong goal has been to help businesses recognize the benefits of integrating the opinions and perceptions of consumers into the development of products and services.

The firm has expertise in comparing customer behavior across cultures and has the ability to make in-depth comparisons of customer satisfaction across a wide range of industries. J.D. Power and Associates' standard quality measurement system, which has since become a benchmark in the automotive industry for measuring the quality of new vehicles, also makes it possible to compare the performance of the industry over time.

Associates at the firm's worldwide headquarters in Westlake Village, California.

While best known for its work in the automotive industry, J.D. Power and Associates has in recent years expanded to serve a number of other industries including travel and hotels, telecommunications, marine, utilities, healthcare, homebuilding, and financial services. Headquartered in Westlake Village, California, the firm's international operations serve more than a dozen other countries.

Today, due largely to the influence of J.D. Power and Associates, manufacturers, service providers, and consumers now have quality and customer satisfaction benchmarks by which to measure and compare products and services across a variety of industries. Consumers can now access these product and service ratings at www.jdpower.com.

INTEGRATED SCANNING OF AMERICA, INC.

Established in 1993, Integrated Scanning of America (I.S.A.) operates as a quality conscious service bureau organization specializing in high volume document capture. Having converted over 160 million pages, this innovative company undertakes medium to large projects with over 150 satisfied clients including Government, Health, Industrial, Financial, Education, and Services.

Serving as one of the top three Southern California microfilm and microfiche to digital conversion shops, I.S.A. is known as one of the most mature, knowledgeable, and comprehensive document image service providers in the county. Using its own innovative technology with unprecedented automation, I.S.A. enjoys an admirable track record and reputation.

I.S.A. was the brainchild of Manuel Bulwa and Isabel Sandez who first began by scanning medical records for a Ventura Hospital. Since then, the company has converted paper and microfilm records for the County of Ventura, the Ventura Unified School District, and many local cities, water districts, and private businesses. I.S.A. delivers CD-ROM, DVD, or other media of the client's choice, and provides Internet secure online repository access for its domestic and international clients wishing to conduct business via the Internet.

By applying its decades of expertise in the industry towards a much better and safer alternative, and sharing this knowledge with the community through educational seminars, I.S.A. has managed to provide a resourceful service to both the community and its residents.

Isabel Sandez and Manuel Bulwa, proud founders of I.S.A.

Photo by John Eder

Photo by John Eder

CALIFORNIA SPINE INSTITUTE

For many years, people with spinal problems had to either endure painful surgery with a long recovery time, or live with the pain. In answer to that problem, the California Spine Institute (CSI) dedicated itself to the practice, research, and development of innovative procedures of minimally invasive spinal surgery, more commonly known as MISS. As home to the California Center for Minimally Invasive Spine Surgery, the California Spine Institute's mission, "less is better; less is more" in spinal care, challenges the concept that open spinal surgery is today's gold standard.

Traditionally, standard open spine surgery, including fusion and discectomy, or disc removal, has been associated with some morbidity and mortality, as well as expensive long-term convalescence. Therefore, CSI began to search for a minimally invasive procedure, one that would not require a large incision, and thereby would not require a long hospital stay. A pioneer in the evolution of MISS is Dr. John C. Chiu, Chief of Neurospine Surgery. He is the founding chairman of the American Academy of Minimally Invasive Spinal Surgery and Medicine, as well as a visiting professor in various countries. He has authored and presented over 300 papers at national and international scientific meetings.

In the emerging field of MISS, Dr. Chiu performed or developed innovative procedures including Microdecompressive Endoscopic Spinal Disc Surgery, Laser Thermodiskoplasty to shrink and to tighten the disc tissue, robot-aided surgery, and decompression of spinal stenosis. As the result of his contributions, he has received numerous honors and awards both nationally and internationally. The advantages for same-day minimally invasive spinal surgery are numerous, including faster recovery, less trauma, and cost savings from shorter hospital stay and shorter time away from work. Even sufferers from chronic and severe back pain can be successfully treated.

CSI works hand in hand with various high tech companies to research and promote MISS technologies. The digital x-ray

California Spine Institute is the home for California Center, Minimally Invasive Spine Surgery, a leader in MISS.

department—one of the first available in the region—provides clearer, faster, better quality images with less x-ray exposure. The California Spine Institute is also home to a futuristic "3D Medical Surgical Planning Laboratory" with the latest ultra fast CT scan and MRI scan, which is open on all four sides to ease the fears of children or claustrophobic patients and virtual 3D scan. It can perform many unusual scans, including non-invasive coronary artery study, angiogram, and non-invasive colonoscopy, thereby avoiding the discomfort of the conventional test.

The ultra-fast CT scan and MRI scan can even provide a wellness scan, which is a total body scan of the chest, abdomen, and pelvis to find any unsuspected tumor, polyp, cyst, hemorrhoid, calcification, or heart disease. With this scan as well as the virtual reality system, surgeons can study a transparent, virtual patient to determine the best approach to surgery before the actual patient ever enters the operating room.

Among other innovations at CSI is the "Institutional Information System" (IIS), a platform for Web-based global telediagnostics, tele-medicine, tele-surgery, and tele-conference that is based on a paperless/filmless system. State-of-the-art digital networking equipment and a complete digital T.V. station provides seamless imaging and networking for the clinical practice, endoscopic surgical suite, rehabilitation center, and a digital medical library, as well as a high tech conference room and VIP room. The California Minimally Invasive Surgery Center provides the most advanced digital endoscopic operating rooms with a modern, high-tech surgical environment for outpatient minimally invasive endoscopic and laser spinal surgery. The latest surgical

Abundance of light, natural materials, and attractive interior décor create a healing environment.

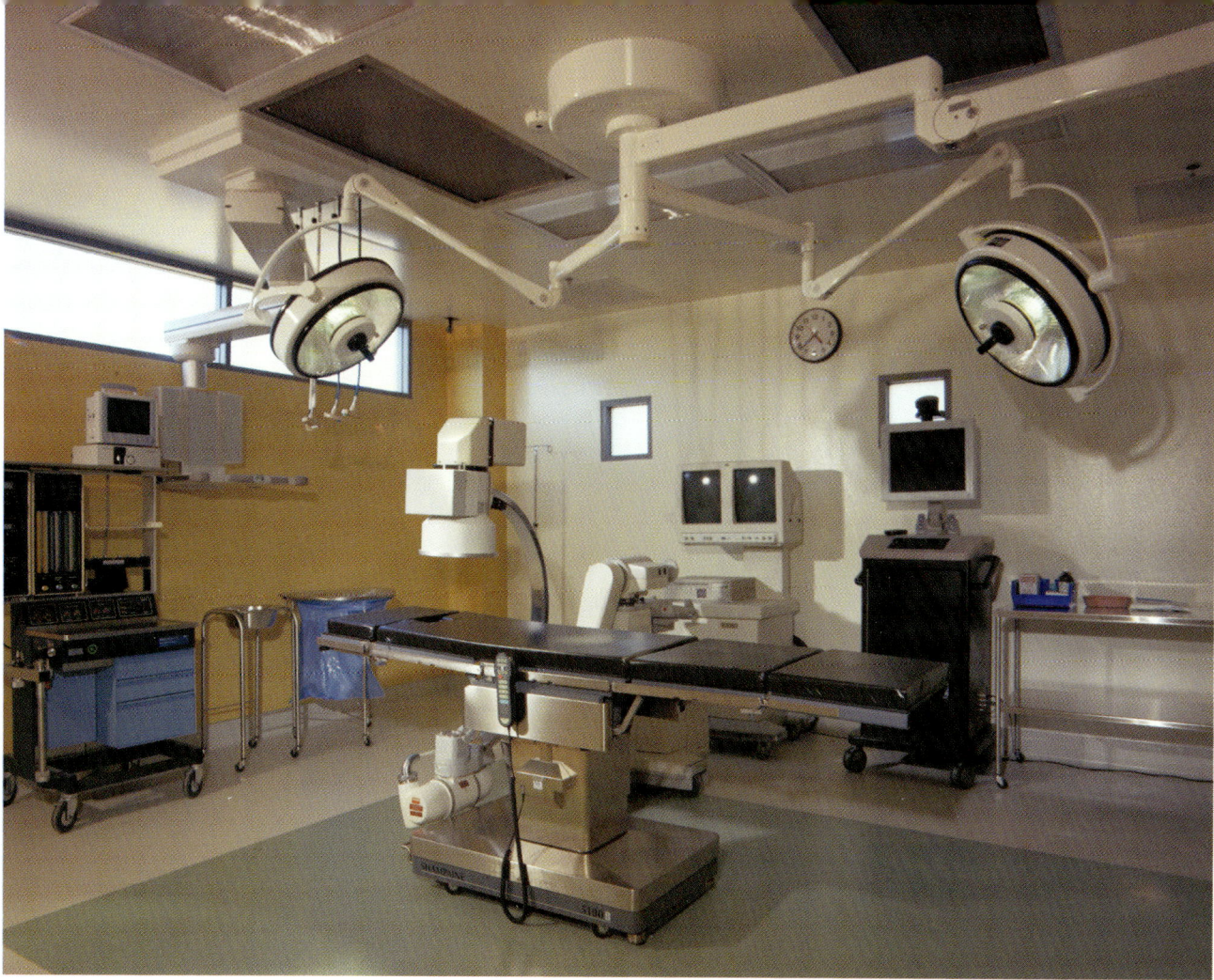

equipment, including surgical robotics, an image guided system, radio frequency system, monitoring equipment, and laser machines enhance the patient's results from outpatient surgery.

The California Spine Institute also provides wellness, rehabilitation, and comprehensive pain management. The Thousand Oaks Spine and Sports Center provides an ultra modern computerized physical medicine department for rehabilitation and back-to-work programs. The facility includes state-of-the-art computerized exercise machines, treadmills, and a digitally monitored motorized pool and sauna, to help restore motion of the joints and spine. The equipment complements the rehabilitation and wellness program, allowing patients to increase strength endurance and functional capacity. A pain management specialist is also on hand to provide a comprehensive pain management program.

California Spinal Institute provides public education and care for spinal patients from the United States and globally. CSI also offers professional programs for education and fellowship training for specialists. CSI has established medical exchange programs with numerous countries, and offers global teleconsultation, telemedicine, and telesurgery, made possible by a digital television station and teleconferencing technology.

The architectural design of the CSI facility is unique, with a distinctive outward structure and attractive interior. Designed to create a healing environment, the facility contains unusual features such as a bamboo meditation garden. CSI is situated in an ecologically minded natural setting, along the bustling bio-technological corridor, Highway 101 in southern California.

California Spinal Institute provides spinal sufferers effective minimally invasive spinal surgery technology and non-fusion technology

A most advanced digital, endoscopic surgical suite equipped with a complete digital T.V. station.

in an ultra-modern facility via a global super digital networking system. This technology and a dedication to patient well-being are what makes CSI center of excellence for spinal patients. Further information is available at www.spinecenter.com. ✄

The CSI combines distinctive art and architecture with technological innovations, all seamlessly connected to the global information super highway.

CALIFORNIA LUTHERAN UNIVERSITY

*S*ilhouetted against the softly rolling hills of Thousand Oaks, the spire on California Lutheran University's Chapel symbolizes the purpose for which the University was founded—to provide an intellectual, spiritual, moral, and cultural environment where students build a solid academic foundation while developing talents and character that lead to lives of effective service in the world.

Since the turn of the century, Lutherans on the West Coast had entertained a dream of an institution of higher learning in California where they could educate their children in the Lutheran tradition and heritage. In 1959 that dream became reality in Thousand Oaks when California Lutheran College was jointly founded by the American Lutheran Church and the Pacific Southwest Synod of the Lutheran Church in America.

The persistence of Lutheran visionaries from throughout the West Coast formed the foundation of the new college, but it was the son of Conejo Valley pioneers who helped convert the founders' dreams into bricks and mortar.

A major portion of the land which forms the campus of California Lutheran University was donated by Richard Pederson. The son of Norwegian immigrants who came to the Conejo Valley in 1890, Pederson desired his 130-acre ranch, which forms the heart of the 290-acre campus, to be used for the educational advancement of the youth of his church, community, and nation. He wanted his land, which had been "lovingly tilled, nurtured, and harvested, to cultivate a new crop—fertile, inquiring minds."

The new college attracted a cadre of well-educated, talented faculty and administrators from all over the nation. This pioneering group of highly committed individuals contributed their time to help build the newly incorporated City of Thousand Oaks. In fact, many of the educational and cultural amenities of the city took root

on the CLU campus, e.g., formation of a community symphony orchestra, establishment of the Arts Council of the Conejo Valley, and promotion of a cultural center that eventuated into the Civic Arts Plaza. Employees and graduates of CLU serve on local city councils, planning commissions, and chamber of commerce executive boards.

Since its founding, CLU, the first four-year comprehensive university in Ventura County, has experienced remarkable growth. From its original class of 330 freshmen and sophomores in September 1961, California Lutheran has become a dynamic, liberal arts and science university with approximately 1,800 undergraduate students and about 1,000 graduate students. The University offers 34 majors within the Schools of Business and Education and the College of Arts and Sciences, five graduate programs, and a new doctoral program. To more accurately reflect the growth in majors and programs, the name of California Lutheran College was changed to University in 1986.

Originating from 37 states and 19 foreign countries, CLU's student body represents a diversity of faiths and cultures. Graduates of California Lutheran University have moved on to become leaders in education and business throughout the nation and the world. The impact of CLU alumni is felt in every aspect of life—in the church and community, in education, business, law, medicine, and the arts.

The impact of CLU is also felt on the economy of the community. As one of the largest employers in the city, the University contributes greatly to the economic viability of the region. In addition, its students provide an ongoing workforce for local businesses, and alumni often remain in the Conejo Valley to establish their businesses and raise their families.

(above) The "Enormous Luther" statue of Martin Luther graces Falde Square on the campus of California Lutheran University.

(below) CLU students enjoy a break between classes outside the Pearson Library and Preus-Brandt Forum.

The University's history of expansion over the years is due in great part to its reputation for high academic standards, an outstanding and involved faculty, its commitment to faith, and its beautiful Southern California location.

The University prides itself on being a community resource serving as a center for community dialogue, academic research and exploration, and professional interaction. CLU is home to KCLU-FM, which provides jazz, news, and NPR favorites to listeners throughout Ventura County (88.3) and Santa Barbara County (102.3).

As the number and scope of classes and programs has grown steadily over the years, so has the University's physical plant. Within the past 15 years, several major structures have been added to the campus: Pearson Library/Preus-Brandt Forum in 1985; the Ahmanson Science Center in 1988; Samuelson Chapel in 1991; the Soiland Humanities Center and Overton Hall in 1998; and the Spies-Bornemann Center for Education and Technology in 2002. Additional residence halls have also been constructed to provide housing for more than a thousand students.

In March 1999, the Thousand Oaks City Council approved CLU's 20-year Master Plan, which calls for replacing most of the original buildings and developing the University's north campus with new athletic facilities. The plan also envisions the growth of the University to 2,200 traditional students.

In its brief history, California Lutheran University has not only expanded its student body and physical plant but, more importantly, has sent a legion of graduates and the children of graduates into the world. Richard Pederson's dream of cultivating minds for effective service in the world has been realized again and again. 🏃

(below) CLU's Samuelson Chapel is silhouetted against the rolling green hills of Thousand Oaks.

(bottom) Students gather at the gazebo in beautiful Kingsmen Park, the center of campus activity.

NORMAN J. NAGEL, D.D.S., M.S.

Dr. Norman J. Nagel has practiced his dental specialty of Orthodontics in the Conejo Valley for almost 30 years. He recognized the area as a safe, family-oriented community—important to a father of four young children. With offices in Thousand Oaks and Simi Valley, Dr. Nagel has continuously provided quality orthodontic care ("braces") to his patients—children as well as adults.

Dr. Nagel received his education at Valparaiso University (Indiana) and earned his B.S., D.D.S., M.S., and Certificate of Postdoctoral Training (Orthodontics) at Case Western Reserve University in Cleveland, Ohio. Following his formal education, he interned at the U.S. Naval Hospital in San Diego, California and completed his military active duty in Pearl Harbor, Hawaii. Dr. Nagel remained active in the military, completing 38 years as a reserve officer with the Naval Reserve and California Army National Guard. He retired from the Guard in 2002 as a Colonel.

Dr. Nagel has also been active in the community and his profession. He has served as an elected Trustee for the Community Colleges of Ventura County and is a Past President of the Thousand Oaks Rotary Club. In dentistry, he is a Past President of the Santa Barbara-Ventura County Dental Society and the California Association of Orthodontists. He has served as the President of his congregation at the Redeemer Lutheran Church and is currently a member of Ascension Lutheran Church. Dr. Nagel was also a founder and Director of California Oaks State Bank. He has consulted for VAMC Los Angeles and Sepulveda and is currently a lecturer at the UCLA School of Dentistry.

Dr. Nagel and his wife Carol enjoy time with their children and grandchildren. They believe that Ventura County is a wonderful area to raise a family and remain active in their church and community. Never one to "slow down," Dr. Nagel and his staff enjoy working with all ages, helping each and every patient achieve a healthier, brighter smile.

Dr. Nagel is also a certified Invisalign provider, providing "invisible" braces to those patients that are able to wear the popular removable appliances.

(above) **Norman J. Nagel, D.D.S., M.S.**

(below) **"When you smile, we smile!"**

"When you smile, we smile," is Dr. Nagel's motto. Treating the children of former patients (when they were children) is a great tribute to the care and attention that Dr. Nagel and his experienced staff provide to their patients.

Above all, Dr. Nagel wishes to thank Conejo Valley for providing he and his staff with 30 wonderful years.

For more information, please visit www.bracesbydrnagel.com.

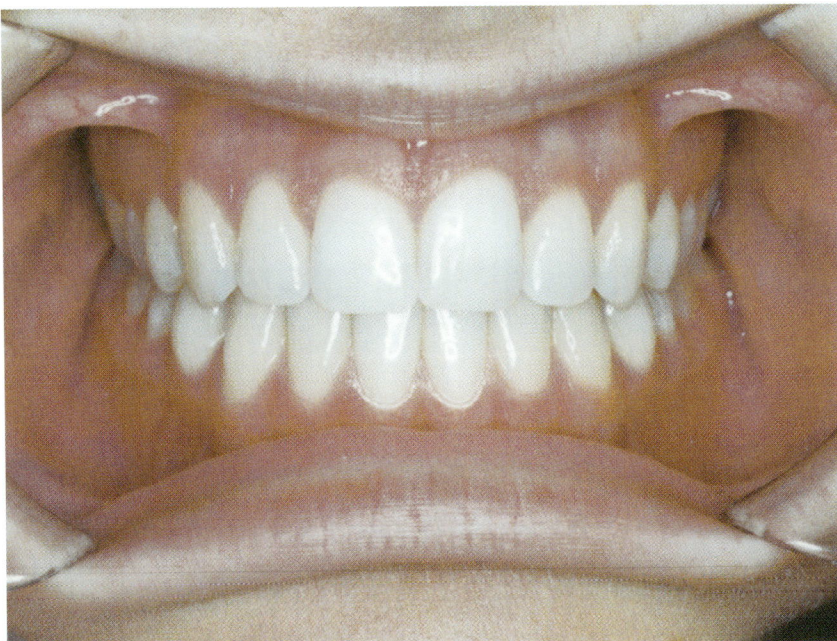

PACIFIC UNION CONFERENCE

The Pacific Union Conference is the western regional head-quarters of the Seventh-day Adventist Church in the Pacific Southwest, serving 750 Adventist Christian congregations and 150 elementary and secondary parochial schools as well as a college and two universities in a five state region which includes California, Arizona, Utah, Nevada, and Hawaii.

Through the years the Pacific Union Conference headquarters has been located in various areas of California. When the staff out-grew its quarters in Glendale, the office was relocated in 1976 to a new building on a more spacious site in the Thousand Oaks/ Westlake Village area. The new facility better met the demands of a growing church membership and was designed to complement the surrounding expanding community.

With between 50 and 100 employees, services provided are pri-marily administrative, assisting leadership of educational institutions, financial services for church members and institutions, and coordi-nation for smaller administrative regions known as local conferences.

Additional services housed at the office include an arm of the world church auditing staff serving Adventist institutions in the Pacific Southwest. The Pacific Union Conference is also home to the Western Adventist Foundation. Its public affairs and religious liberty staff actively pursues the protection of individual rights, not only for Adventist members but for the public at large. In addition to serving Caucasian congregations, the conference staff includes

This three-story office building is the administrative headquarters for the Seventh-day Adventist church in five Pacific Southwest states.

ethnic ministries coordinators who provide leadership for scores of churches representing Hispanic, Asian, and African American nationalities. ✳

Photo by John Eder

Photo by John Eder

GARRETT INTERIORS, INC.

For nearly 30 years, Garrett Interiors has served the Conejo Valley area as an exemplary design service firm, establishing an unmatched reputation for providing cost-effective and tasteful designs for all levels of business and residential interiors and exteriors. Utilizing a staff that is credentialed and trained in all aspects of residential and commercial design, Garrett Interiors thrives on helping people and companies of all income levels achieve exquisite, yet comfortable design in an industry that is sometimes viewed as exclusive and overpriced.

Sandy Garrett founded the business in the early 1970s as Garrett and Yops Interiors, based on her married and maiden name. Sandy was searching to fill a void in the Conejo Valley as a business that offered creative items with personalized service for the rising number of new homes being built in the area. The business was started in Westlake Village due to the community being carefully planned with stores, shopping areas and commercial buildings easily accessible to local residences. Word of mouth proved to be the ideal advertising method as Garrett and Yops Interiors quickly became known for the dedication and benefit that it brought to each of its customers homes. The business soon became an established and widely recognized design firm in the area whose work was published in builder magazines such as *California Homes, Southern California Builder, Builder/Architect* magazine as well as model home designs in trade magazines and widespread coverage on television.

In January 2002, Sandy sold the business to Karen Dry who retained Sandy's services as an in-demand designer and shortened

Garrett Interiors employees. Photo by Mark Brandes Photography

The showroom/gallery of Garrett Interiors. Photo by Bill Upston Photography

the name of the business to Garrett Interiors Inc., which helped serve a broader base, speaking well to both the men and women in the design industry. Today, Garrett Interiors prospers from its reputation based on Sandy's longevity in the area and has become well known for having the most exquisite design gallery in the community. Stretching across 4,800 square feet of space, the Garrett Interiors gallery features resplendent furniture, lighting, custom rugs, and accessories with a unique resource library that is completely accessible to its customers. Garrett Interiors offers over 65,000 fabrics, wallpaper, trims, carpet, furniture, molding, flooring, and lighting samples providing a complete design experience. By allowing the customer access to every facet of the process, each customer walks away satisfied not only with their purchases but with the complete customer service that Garrett Interiors provides.

Garrett Interiors has never been exclusive in its customer base. The company has helped design homes in nearly every economical setting from the average neighbor on your street to legendary actor Mickey Rooney. It has designed rooms in design houses in North Ranch, Toluca Lake, and Palm Springs as well as corporations such as Griffen Communities, Fiesta Homes, Baskin Robbins, Rampage Clothing Stores, Silagi Development, and Sares-Regis. By not restraining the business to just one atmosphere such as French country or contemporary, Garrett Interiors has opened its doors to a wide array of ideas, designs, and solutions for every room that it's called upon to assist. By having so many talented designers with several different backgrounds in one place, each customer has a choice in the type of design that they are searching for and finding the right designer for their respective projects. And thanks

the help of many local builders, carpenters, and subcontractors, which are then displayed at a local mall. After a two-month viewing process by the public, the playhouses are then auctioned off for charity, usually bringing in nearly $50,000 for each one. The proceeds from Project Playhouse are then put towards building temporary housing for displaced families throughout the community.

In addition to its charity work, Karen Dry has also served as the President of two local marketing groups that are associated with the Chamber of Commerce—the Westlake marketing group and the Agoura Business Network International group. Sandy Garrett has served as the vice president of the Conejo Association of Professional Interior Designers as well in the past.

Throughout the years, Garrett Interiors has continued to thrive in the design community because of the diversity of designs that it offers and its commitment to excellence—excellence not only in the varied design services that the company provides, but also in the way that it manages each of its relationships with its customers. The customer's success is also the company's success—something that Garrett Interiors will never forget for a moment. 🪶

to the technology implemented by Garrett Interiors, the business can offer its services to clients who have multiple homes.

As the community has been so receptive to Garrett Interiors, Garrett Interiors has taken care of its community in several different ways. The company is involved with several different community volunteer efforts such as the Women's Council, which is associated with the national Builders Industry Association (BIA) that organizes several functions throughout each year. One of those functions is related to HomeAid, called Project Playhouse. The goal of the organization is to build fully functional playhouses for children with

Sample of Garrett Interiors' work in a residential dining room. Photo by Bill Upston Photography

North Ranch Showcase House.

OAKWOOD WORLDWIDE

Oakwood Worldwide is the leading global provider of furnished apartments, providing delightful accommodations to serve the needs of business travelers, relocating executives, and others in need of temporary housing, such as people in-between homes.

"We want to thank you for the wonderful way you treated us," wrote M. Alexander, a recent guest of Oakwood in Los Angeles. "There is so much about Oakwood we will miss; not just the facility itself, but also the feeling of community and interaction (with the staff) that we both enjoyed." Alexander's words encapsulate the guest experience which Oakwood strives to deliver to every resident.

(above) Oakwood Marina del Rey, just one of Oakwood's many properties in the Greater Los Angeles area.

(below) The inside of a furnished Oakwood corporate apartment.

A perfect home away-from-home, Oakwood offers beautifully decorated apartments with furniture, linens, cookware, home electronics, phone, and cable. The atmosphere is more residential than a hotel. Rather than having to dodge hordes of hotel guests, the discerning Oakwood client can simply go home, stretch out on their couch, and relax in the comfort of their own apartment.

In the greater Los Angeles area, Oakwood offers more than 3,000 apartment homes, including prime locations in Beverly Hills, Burbank/Toluca Lake, Woodland Hills, Marina del Rey, Pasadena, Santa Monica, Sherman Oaks, Seal Beach, Thousand Oaks, Torrance, Westlake Village, Westwood, and more. Guests contact Oakwood's Web site www.oakwood.com to arrange the location they desire.

In the Conejo Valley, the firm owns Oakwood Thousand Oaks, a 154-unit luxury apartment property located at 351 Hodencamp Road. The beautiful complex features French country architecture and handsome tree-lined landscaping. Its location is under five minutes drive from numerous restaurants, the Thousand Oaks Mall, the 101 Freeway, and the Moorpark Freeway (Route 23). Both furnished and unfurnished apartments are available. Each of the residences at Oakwood Thousand Oaks offers its own washer/dryer, refrigerator/freezer, dishwasher, covered parking, wall-to-wall carpeting, and large private balconies. Oakwood Thousand Oaks also features a heated swimming pool and whirlpool spa with mountain view sundeck; resident barbecue area; and professionally equipped fitness center.

Ever since Chairman Howard Ruby and two partners founded L.A.-based Oakwood Worldwide in 1960, the company philosophy has been to provide apartments with something extra in the way of amenities, furnishings and personal service. A huge clientele has responded to Oakwood's housing innovations, and the growing list of customers now includes Fortune 500 corporations, the entertainment industry, professional sports teams, government and military personnel, small businesses, leisure travelers, families, and seniors. Oakwood Worldwide is continuing to grow its business in both Southern California and around the globe—the company now has locations throughout the U.S., U.K., and Asia too. Ruby's philosophy is to constantly enhance the guest experience at his properties and build long-term relationships with his clients.

"Our goal is nothing short of a perfect apartment every time," says Ruby.

THE HAALAND GROUP

Since 1971, the Haaland Group has been providing its clients with innovative and unique solutions to their sophisticated development projects in a responsive and environmentally-sensitive manner. Working together, this dedicated team of professional civil engineers, land planners, architects, and surveyors has built a reputation out of salvaging projects which had previously been thought destined to fail by its clients.

The Haaland Group, founded by the late Robert S. Haaland, achieves success where others fail by relying on several key factors that are applied to each project that is presented to the company. By employing hard work, integrity, accountability, continuous learning, excellence in planning, and open, ongoing communication, the Haaland Group has helped distinguish itself as not only a trusted resource but a leader in the field of project development and design.

Through the nurturing of relationships with independent professionals who excel in their respective fields, the Haaland Group has developed an extensive network of traffic engineers, architects, environmental advisors, landscape engineers, structural engineers, and experts in soils and geology. These experts are made available to the Haaland Group's clients, offering fresh and unprecedented ideas that benefit both the client and the company.

The Haaland Group thrives on challenges and scrutinizes each project carefully in order to preserve the client's vision of the finished product, turning those visions into realities. The Company has successfully accumulated several signature projects that have helped define the Haaland Group as a company that is able to conquer obstacles. Dos Vientos Ranch in Thousand Oaks faced not only topographic restrictions and infrastructure constraints but was facing opposition by local community and powerful environmentalist groups when the Haaland Group first took on the project. Through an inclusive process, the Company was able to overcome these strong objections, uniting both groups' diverging interests, keeping the project on-track, and produced one of the more beautiful planned communities in Thousand Oaks.

(above) Entrance to the Prestigious Lake Sherwood Country Club.

(below) The Haaland Team.

Another project that was able to showcase the Haaland Group's talents was the Blue Rock Country Club in Hayward. For 12 years, three different civil engineering firms had failed to solve the complex hillside grading issues that had been complicated by sensitive environmental obstructions. The Haaland Group took over the project and within a year had found a creative solution and entitled an 18-hole Cal Olson designed championship golf course surrounded by 615 homes, ultimately saving the client over $4 million in grading costs alone.

These are just two examples of the hundreds of projects that the Haaland Group has been called upon to resurrect, turning trouble-plagued plans into successful ventures with the dedication and the heart that has propelled the Company for over 30 years.

PAT HELTON, CRS, GRI—REAL ESTATE BROKER

"Unique and creative." "Innovative and passionate about her profession." These are just a few of the comments that satisfied clients have made about Pat Helton. Providing excellence in action, Pat Helton is one of the most successful real estate brokers in the Conejo Valley, taking pride in providing the most superior of real estate services to each of her clients.

A long time resident of the Conejo Valley, Pat has been a licensed Realtor in California since 1985 after discovering an opportunity to provide the American Dream for residents of the area. Specializing in selling properties from townhomes to estates in the Conejo Valley, Pat's areas of expertise are Thousand Oaks, Westlake Village, Newbury Park, Agoura Hills Moorpark, Simi Valley and Calabasas, placing hundreds of happy families in the finest of homes.

Pat's background as an educator has proven beneficial in her real estate career. For 10 years, she gave students the necessary tools to assist them in achieving their personal goals. "Teaching comes natural to me," she says. "I take the time to help people fully understand concepts so they can make informed decisions."

This approach to her occupation has helped make her one of the most recognizable names in residential real estate in the Conejo Valley. By not viewing herself as a salesperson, but rather as a counselor, facilitator and expert business person who helps people make wise financial decisions with their most important investment, Pat has earned the respect and confidence of each family with which she's worked.

Pat's greatest strengths lie in her ability to communicate effectively and to listen carefully to her client's needs in order to best service them. Her professional excellence and unparalleled service have catapulted her to more than $250 million in sales and a standing as a consistent top broker in the Thousand Oaks area for almost two decades.

Firmly believing in giving back to the community that has given so much to her, Pat is a generous donor to local schools, charities,

(above) Pat Helton, CRS, GRI-Real Estate Broker providing the American dream since 1985!

(below) Pat Helton and her husband, John, are long-time residents of Westlake Village and enjoy boating, biking, and hiking throughout the Conejo Valley.

and the theater. She also remains active in many local organizations such as the Westlake/Thousand Oaks Chamber of Commerce, American Association of University Women, and the Alliance for the Arts.

Providing personalized service and superior client care with excellent success in repeat referral business, Pat Helton is able to put families on the road to achieving their real estate goals, accumulating a phenomenal track record in the process. Which is why many residents agree that Pat Helton is the only name buyers and sellers need to remember in the Conejo Valley.

For more information visit www.PatHelton.com. 🏇

Photo by John Eder

Chapter Eleven

11

The Marketplace, Entertainment & Tourism

Photo by John Eder

THE THOUSAND OAKS AUTO MALL

The Thousand Oaks Auto Mall began 35 years ago, in September 1967, with the construction of the first dealership, Courtesy Chevrolet. Now, three decades and 13 dealerships later, the Thousand Oaks Auto Mall carries the largest selection of vehicles in the world, offering a selection of 32 makes in one location. The Thousand Oaks Auto Mall prides itself for its easy comparison shopping, competitive prices, incentives, central location, friendly service, no pressure sales, quality maintenance and repair, and a strong commitment to community service. In fact, for every vehicle sold or leased at the Thousand Oaks Auto Mall, money is donated to help fund vital programs at local schools.

Located just off the 101 freeway at the Westlake exit, the Thousand Oaks Auto Mall is just minutes from anywhere in the San Fernando Valley, Conejo Valley, or Ventura County. And for those who live a little further away, it's still worth the drive, considering the convenience of its one-stop comparison shopping and exceptionally competitive prices.

The list of vehicle makes available at the Thousand Oaks Auto Mall includes Audi, BMW, Buick, Cadillac, Chevrolet, Chrysler, Dodge, Ford, GMC Truck, Honda, Hummer, Infiniti, Jaguar, Jeep, Land Rover, Lexus, Lincoln/Mercury, Lotus, Mazda, Mercedes, Mitsubishi, Nissan, Pontiac, Porsche, Saab, Saturn, Subaru, Volkswagen, and Volvo.

Growing from just one dealership to its present position as a heavy player in the economic structure of the city, the Thousand Oaks Auto Mall represents how a group of businesses can bond together for success. As a key player in the city's economy, the Thousand Oaks Auto Mall offers over 1,000 jobs, contributing approximately 25 percent of the city's sales tax base. The Thousand Oaks Auto Mall is also well known as a major source of support for the local community.

With an eye on the future, the Thousand Oaks Auto Mall is constantly reviewing and analyzing its position in the community for charitable contributions.

In January 1999, the Thousand Oaks Auto Mall began supporting six cash starved local elementary schools by pledging funds for each vehicle sold for items such as books, computer-assisted reading programs, and to furnish computers for each classroom. To date the

Front row (left to right): David Pierce, Rusnak-Westlake; Susan Mejia, Silver Star Automotive Group; Jeff Kem, Kemp Ford; Ken Greene, Silver Star Motor Car Company; Howie Neftin, Neftin Westlake Car Company; Chris Shaver, Shaver Automotive Group. Back row (left to right) John Woodward III, Westoaks Chrysler/Dodge; Steve Gleason, Mazda, Subaru & Suzuki Thousand Oaks; A.J. Patterson, Westlake Motors; Irv Steinman, Silver Star Automotive Group; Bill Little, Silver Star Automotive Group; John McClure, Courtesy Chevrolet. Not pictured: Steve Lapin, Infiniti of Thousand Oaks; Gordon Chu, Saturn of Thousand Oaks.

Auto Mall has donated over half a million dollars. Employees are also paid their hourly wage to volunteer at local elementary schools on a variety of projects, from reading to students to assisting with homework.

The Thousand Oaks Auto Mall regularly contributes to dozens of charitable causes including MANNA, Many Mansions, Senior Concerns, the Boy Scouts, Girl Scouts, Rotary Clubs, the Chamber of Commerce, and numerous elementary, junior, and high school programs.

With all its history and success over the years, the Thousand Oaks Auto Mall has rightfully garnered a top position in the city and looks forward to enjoying many more years of growth and service to the local community.

HOGAN FAMILY FOUNDATION

Tourism has always been cited as one of the key ingredients to the success of any local or state economy. Philanthropists Ed and Lynn Hogan have worked in the tourism industry for several decades as the proprietors of Pleasant Holidays, the largest tour operator to Hawaii and both fully understand the value that tourism has on a community. Acknowledging the rewarding success that the couple has achieved throughout their 40 years in the travel business, the Hogans' set a goal a few years ago to be able to give back to their community and the world as a whole through a variety of charitable programs. This goal resulted in the creation of the Hogan Family Foundation.

First formed in 1998, the Hogan Family Foundation is a non profit operating organization, a 501(c)(3) whose mission is to promote a greater understanding of the importance of travel and tourism within our society and the world as a whole by creating and operating educational, humanitarian, and civic-minded programs that encourage meaningful communication among people of all cultures.

One of those programs is the Gardens of the World in Thousand Oaks. This 4.5-acre community park is located across the street from the Thousand Oaks Civic Arts Plaza in the heart of the community and serves as a beautiful monument commemorating the various cultures of the world. The Gardens of the World Community Park has added to the beauty of the community and provides an educational benefit to the children of the Conejo Valley. The City of Thousand Oaks was very supportive of this development and lent its support in many different ways.

Another of the Foundation's programs is the Children's Foster Care Support Program in which the Foundation provides "My Bag" filled with necessities to children in foster care homes in Ventura County. The Foundation also holds annual events during the year to entertain these children.

(above) **The French Fountain at the Gardens of the World Community Park in Thousand Oaks.**

(below) **Glenn, Chris, Ed, Lynn, Gary, and Brian Hogan.**

Other programs offered by the Foundation include educational ventures such as the Hogan Entrepreneurial Program at Chaminade University; the Hogan Entrepreneurial Leadership Program at Gonzaga University; and a mobile classroom that houses educational information concerning career opportunities available in the fields of travel and tourism. The Foundation has also given birth to such successful projects as the HEART Program and the Hogan Angel Flight Program to name just a few.

The Hogan Family Foundation hopes to continue as a successful and productive operating foundation thus leaving an indelible mark on the community as a whole. 🦋

THE OAKS SHOPPING CENTER

The Oaks Shopping Center, built in 1978, is situated on 90 acres of land and has established itself as the premier location for shopping in the Conejo Valley.

With 1.3 million square feet of shopping, the center offers residents traditional department stores such as Macy's, Robinsons-May, and JCPenney, along with over 130 national and local retailers and an eclectic mix of dining including Sisley Italian Kitchen and The Cheesecake Factory. More than 5 million shoppers visit the center each year helping make The Oaks one of the most popular shopping destinations in the area.

Purchased in June of 2002 by the Macerich Company, future plans for the shopping center include focusing on providing the community with a destination for shopping that offers a quality experience, convenience, and an exceptional selection of stores. Most important is the Macerich Company's dedication to creating shopping centers that are committed to the communities in which they do business.

The Oaks Shopping Center offers a variety of stores, making it a place for ideal shopping.

Photo by John Eder

BIBLIOGRAPHY

Anderson, Charles A. et al. *1940 E.W. Scripps Cruise to the Gulf of California, Memoir 43.* New York: Geological Society of America, 1950.

Chrisman, Harry E. *1001 Most-Asked Questions About the American West.* N.p.: Swallow Press, 1982.

Christman, Margaret C.S. *1846: Portrait of a Nation.* Washington: Smithsonian, 1996.

Fabricius, Klaus and Red Saunders, eds. *24 Hours in the Life of Los Angeles.* New York: Alfred van der Marck, 1984.

Gudde, Erwin G. *1000 California Place Names: The Story Behind the Naming of Mountains, Rivers, Lakes, Capes, Bays, Counties, and Cities.* Berkeley: Univ. of California Press, 1971.

Hopkins, Henry Profuse. *50 West Coast Artists.* San Francisco: Chronicle Books, 1981.

Institute of California History Foundation. 17th Annual Report. 1964.

Mahood, Ruth I. The 20 Dioramas of California History in the California Hall of the Los Angeles County Museum of History and Science. Los Angeles County Museum, 1965.

Thousand Oaks Star/ Ventura County Star archives.

Thousand Oaks-Westlake Village Chamber of Commerce, Web site and publications.

Wells, Evelyn and Harry C. Peterson. *The 49'ers: Facts and Tall Tales From the Fabulous Days of '49.* Garden City: Doubleday, 1949.

Young, Bob and Jan Young. *49'ers: The Story Of The California Gold Rush.* New York: Messner, 1966.

ENTERPRISE INDEX

Market Scan Information Systems, Inc.
31416 Agoura Road, Suite 110
Westlake Village, California 91361
Phone: 818-575-2000
        800-658-7226
Fax: 818-707-8339
E-mail: shamburger@marketscan.com
www.marketscan.com
Page 77

Norman J. Nagel, D.D.S., M.S.
47 Duesenberg Drive, #202
Thousand Oaks, California 91362
Phone: 805-496-5114
Fax: 805-379-3398
E-mail: nagelwire@aol.com
www.bracesbydrnagel.com
Page 92

The Oaks Shopping Center
222 West Hillcrest Drive
Thousand Oaks, California 91360
Phone: 805-495-4628
Fax: 805-495-9656
E-mail: cris_bremner@macerich.com
www.shoptheoaksmall.com
Page 107

Oakwood Worldwide
2222 Corinth Avenue
Los Angeles, California 90064
Phone: 800-888-0808
Fax: 310-444-2210
E-mail: oakwood@oakwoodworldwide.com
www.oakwood.com
Page 98

Pacific Union Conference
2686 Townsgate Road
Box 5005
Westlake Village, California 91359
Phone: 805-497-9457
Fax: 805-495-2644
E-mail: comdept@puconline.org
www.puconline.org
Page 93

Pat Helton, CRS, GRI-Real Estate Broker
171 Thousand Oaks Boulevard, #171
Thousand Oaks, California 91360
Phone: 805-531-4186
Fax: 805-494-0896
E-mail: pat@pathelton.com
www.pathelton.com
Page 100

The Thousand Oaks Auto Mall
3905 Auto Mall Drive
Thousand Oaks, California 91362
Phone: 805-371-5400
Fax: 805-371-5451
E-mail: bcharney@mosaicnet.com
www.thousandoaksautomall.com
Pages 104-105

The Thousand Oaks-Westlake Village Regional Chamber of Commerce
600 Hampshire Road, Suite 200
Westlake Village, California 91361
Phone: 805-370-0035
Fax: 805-370-1083
E-mail: info@towlvchamber.org
www.towlvchamber.org
Pages 80-81

Vivitar Corporation
1280 Rancho Conejo Boulevard
Newbury Park, California 91320
Phone: 805-498-7008
Fax: 805-498-5943
E-mail: gcvivitar@aol.com
www.vivitar.com
Pages 74-75

I N D E X